MEET GOD

Peter Anderson

AMBASSADOR

BELFAST, NORTHERN IRELAND
GREENVILLE, SOUTH CAROLINA

Meet God
© 2002 Peter Anderson

ISBN 1   84030 119 8

Ambassador Books
an imprint of
Ambassador Productions Ltd.
Providence House
Ardenlee Street,
Belfast,
BT6 8QJ
Northern Ireland
www.ambassador-productions.com

Emerald House
427 Wade Hampton Blvd.
Greenville
SC 29609, USA
www.emeraldhouse.com

INTRODUCTION

It was C.S.Lewis who said that, "Over the lives of some people at the end of life's journey could be written the words, 'fine performance, but you missed the whole point'" And one of the major reasons for such a sad epitaph is that for many people the making of a living has become much more important than the making of a life. So much time is spent in wheeling and dealing, scraping and scheming, selling and buying, that some of the most important things in life that are intangible but nevertheless very real are totally neglected. Jesus gave us a solemn warning about this when he said, *'What good will it be for a man if he gains the whole world, yet forfeits his soul.'(Matt. 16:26.)*

As you look out on the world in which we live it certainly does seem to be in a mess as far as the making of a life is concerned. Richard Halverson has described man as 'making out when circumstances are congenial, but crawling when life tumbles in.' Young people are often frustrated when after years of study they are unable to get a job. Workers get bored with their life when they feel themselves to be just cogs in a vast industrial machine that is so impersonal, and older folk feel unwanted. Our whole civilisation seems to be in the unhappy position of the aeroplane pilot who when asked by one of the passengers where are we, replied, 'At the moment we are lost, but we are making good time.' Ann Landers writing in the Reader's Digest said, 'No one puts it in so many words, but there is a viewpoint today that we might as well live it up fast, because to-morrow never comes'. So who does have the answers as to the making of a life that is genuinely satisfying ?

Charles Darwin the founding father of evolution said that, 'Man is the product of a continual and eternal process of evolution' - and so suggests that the making of a life is purely accidental. Sigmund Freud's view of life was that 'Man is a guilt ridden, semi-civilised savage, desperately trying to adjust to life and never quite succeeding.'

The late Bertrand Russell said that, 'Man's origin is but the outcome of an accidental collection of atoms.' He then went on to say that 'No fire, no heroism, no intensity of thought and feeling can preserve an individual life beyond the grave...all the labours of the ages, all the devotion, all the inspiration, all the noonday brightness of human genius are destined to extinction, and when I die, I shall rot.' Playwright Tenessee Williams had an equally nihilistic view of life for he wrote, 'There is a horror in things and our existence is meaningless.'

We live in a scientific age, but can science provide the meaning to life that we look for ? Science has enabled man to travel to the moon and bridge vast distances in space, but science cannot bridge the problems that man so often has with his fellow man. Science can blow up bridges and even mend broken bodies, but it cannot mend broken hearts. Science can take the stains out of clothes, but science cannot erase a guilty conscience. There are deep dimensions of life that are completely outside the jurisdiction of science. So what is the answer ?

In order to be able to make a life as distinct from just making a living we need to meet the God who gave us life in the first place. When a man or woman meets up with God then they meet up with the One who alone has the answers and who can impart the inward strength and power to enable them to make a life that is first of all pleasing to God, and then secondly, satisfying and fulfilling as far as the individual is concerned. But first of all you must meet God, and you can only meet God in Jesus Christ...and it is only then that you will start to make a life as distinct from just making a living...and I hope that as you read this book that you will have such a meeting with the living God.

CONTENTS

CHAPTER ONE

Meet God in the Commandments

All good societies and organisations have laws of association. Families that are loving and secure also have a certain number of accepted standards of behaviour. So if our world is God's creation, and I believe that it is, and if human beings are God's creation, placed upon earth by God their Creator, then it is only reasonable to suppose that God gave instructions to them for the well being of their lives. God has not left us in the dark to muddle through. He has given us an all embracing declaration of what he requires, and it is found in the Bible in the book of Exodus and chapter 20, and it is called the Ten Commandments -and please note to start with that they are not just hints for a happy lifestyle. If God had wanted us to have a permissive society he would have given us Ten Suggestions, but He didn't. He gave us Ten Commandments.

There was a time when most of us could at least recite these laws of God, even if we did not always obey them, but I would hazard a guess that most of to-day's generation would only have a hazy idea about them.

Now it is very interesting when you read the Commandments of God in the Bible *(Exodus 20),* that before one of them is mentioned there is a very important prefix that simply says, *'God spoke all these words.'* In other words the Ten Commandments have not been invented by man as a reasonable code of conduct. Nor were they the result of a committee meeting deciding what might be a helpful code of conduct for society to adhere to. They have been given by God. We are dealing with His law, and they are infinitely important because they are the expression of the character of God.

Man can only approach God on His terms. There can be no mediation between God and man except that which God has laid down as the right way to come to Him. Whenever man tries to establish his own way to God, he ends up establishing his own will, fulfilling his own lusts, and finally living himself as if he was God. It is also important to notice in Exodus 20 that it says that God spoke *'all these words.'* Most people will go along with some of them as summed up by Jesus when he said, *'Love your neighbour as yourself:'* But we cannot and dare not pick and choose which ones suit us. We need to remember that God spoke all of them. The God who said, *'Love your neighbour as yourself.'* also said, *'Love the Lord your God with all your heart and soul and strength.' (Mark 12:30.31.)* You see the law of God was not given to us to praise, it was given to us to be practised !

Three things are necessary for a good law.

First of all **Wisdom** is a priority, and God certainly has this necessary quality. Paul wrote several letters in the New Testament to a young man named Timothy, and in one of them he speaks of the *'only wise God.' (1 Tim.1:17.)* In Colossians 2:3 Paul writes that *'in Christ are hidden all the treasures of wisdom and knowledge.'* God is not the slightest degree baffled and bewildered by what perplexes us. He is either a present help in time of trouble, or He is not much help at all. But He is a help because He is all wise.

Secondly, **Authority** is needed to implement the law in terms of the apprehension and punishment of those who break the law. God has supreme authority because He created all and sustains all. He also sees beyond the outward appearance because the Bible says that *'God looks on the heart.' (1 Sam.16:7)* God is not always a God of immediate justice, but He is a God of ultimate justice. For as long as there is eternity, God has enough time to reckon with those who have rebelled against His rightful authority.

Thirdly, **Permanence** is also required. Jesus said of the law of God that, *'It is easier for heaven and earth to disappear than for the least stroke of a pen to drop out of the law.' (Luke 16:17.)* It was J.C.Ryle a former Bishop of Liverpool who said, ' I cannot find a syllable in the Apostle's writings which teach that any one of the Ten Commandments is done away with. I believe that the coming of Christ's gospel did not alter the position of the Commandments even by one hair's breadth.'

And because *'God spoke all these words,'* a number of things should follow.

We should first of all listen to them. In the New Testament God speaks and says, *'We must pay more careful attention to what we have heard'*. We should certainly not read them and then forget them. We should also treat them with great respect because they are God's words. When God first gave them to the Israelites through Moses he said, 'Take to heart all the words of this law.' *(Deut.32:46)* They are not just for information, they are clear, direct instructions from God that call for obedience. Vance Havner an old American preacher said that, 'We have not learned the Commandments until we obey them.' Sadly, I think that it would be true to say that the majority of people don't respect them, let alone obey them, and society is the poorer because of it.

We live in an age when people do not want to be ruled. The majority think of themselves as responsible adults and say, 'Surely we can leave it to common sense how we live and behave!' But sad to say, sense isn't that common to-day.

On the surface they do appear to major on the negative. But when you look at them in depth you will see that they all have a positive application, and you can change every one of them into a positive blessing. For example the Eighth Commandment says, *'You shall not steal.'* If this command was obeyed what a different, positive society we would live in with the fear of burglary, mugging and stealing from shops and stores removed. Equally the same could be said of the Tenth Commandment that states, 'You shall not covet.' Covetousness is the source of so many problems in our society and also in our personal lives, but what a different world it would be if covetousness was rooted out of our lives !

Then of course there are some people who say that these Commandments are old fashioned and out of date - but so is love, and we don't despise love even if there is so little of it about in our world today.

Others do not want God's Commandments because they spell out an absolute morality and we want a relative morality that can be changed to suit the occasion. It was Karl Hess the philosopher who said that 'Each man is a sovereign entity, with his primary allegiance only to himself' Sadly to-day the doctrine of individual responsibility has been undercut by the theory of evolution which says amongst other things that man is what an evolving world has made him. Man is no longer thought of as a guilty creature, it is his environment that is guilty. So society and man's environment is often blamed for the conduct of delinquents and criminals. In such a scheme of things, the lawless are absolved from guilt, and the guilty are made innocent! However J.B.Philips, a modern Bible translator, wrote that, 'It is the straight edge of God's law that shows us how crooked we are.' Make no mistake about it, God spoke all these words contained in the Ten Commandments and they spell out for us what God requires from us. They may seem narrow, but then so does every airport runway around the world. Yet no passenger wants his pilot to miss that narrow runway and land a few yards off the mark in some field, river, or even a block of flats.

God's Commandments also give us a definition of sin. In the Bible we are told quite clearly that, *'transgression of the law is sin.' (Rom.4:15.)* and until people realise that they are sinners, they will not want to get straightened out. C.H. Spurgeon said, 'The law stirs the mud at the bottom of the pool and proves how foul the waters are, for God's law was given to reveal sin and not to remove it.' In addition the Commandments give us an understanding of what God is like, and one very clear thing from them is that they make quite clear that God has very high standards and demands recognition and adherence to them.

But what are these laws for ?

If you take time to look at them as set out in the Bible *(Exodus 20)* you will notice two very distinctive things about them. God comes first in all of them and they are all personal. Although given centuries ago, they are up to date and deal in a most practical and relevant way with our society today and our place in it.

But possibly one of the most challenging things about God's Commandments is that they deal with the thought life and not just our actions. The Bible says *'As a man thinks in his heart, so is he,'* and Jesus in applying the Commandments for today singles out two of them with devastating effect.

First of all he highlights the Sixth Commandment that says, *'You shalt not kill'* and applies it by saying, *'You have heard that it was said to the people long ago, do not murder, and anyone who murders will be subject to the judgement. But I tell you that anyone who is angry with his brother will be subject to the judgement.' (Matt.5:21,22)*

Secondly, Jesus reminds them of the Seventh Commandment, *'You have heard it said, do not commit adultery. But I tell you that anyone who looks at a woman lustfully has already committed adultery with her in his heart.' (Matt. 7:27,28.)* Such a challenge tells us that God has very high standards of morality and we do well to recognise them. God is love and law is the way He loves us. But it is also true that God is law and love is the way that He rules us, and this is always for our good.

Each Commandment forbids not only the sin itself, but also sins of a similar nature. When the Commandment says, *'You shall not kill.'* it also means that you are not to half kill someone ! In fact you could say that this Commandment forbids all cruelty to human beings. You shall not steal not only applies to other people's property, but also to their reputations.

Jesus puts the challenge.

One day in the life of Jesus when he had been answering the questions of the people, one of the Pharisees, an expert in the law, tested him with a question. *'Teacher, which is the greatest commandment in the law?' Jesus* replied that *'It was to love the Lord your God with all your heart, and with all your soul and with all your mind, This is the first and greatest commandment: and the second is like it: Love your neighbour as yourself.' (Matt.22:37,38.)* Love for God must always take priority over love for man. Don't think that by doing your duty to your neighbour that you have arrived. Unless you love God with all your heart, soul and mind, then you are guilty of breaking the first and greatest commandment. Love to God and obedience to God are so completely involved in each other that any one of them implies the other too. What is even more shattering is that God says, *'For whoever keeps the whole law and yet stumbles at just one point is guilty of breaking all of it.' (James 2:10.)* The same God who forbids murder, also forbids stealing and lying. To disobey the authority at one point is to disobey the authority which stands behind it all. A newspaper reported an unusual incident in a fast food restaurant. The manager had put the day's takings in a paper bag for depositing that night in a bank safe box. However a new worker mistook it for an order and gave it to a couple at the drive -through window. A short time later when the man and woman opened the bag in a nearby park, they were shocked by the contents and immediately drove back to return the money. In the meantime the manager had reported a robbery and a police car and a TV crew were already on the scene. The manager was so relieved to get the money back and said to the couple, 'You will be on the TV local news tonight for your honesty.' 'O please, no publicity,' replied the man nervously 'she's not my wife !' To be honest with another's money, but dishonest with somebody else's wife is not being consistent. Those who go against the grain of God's laws, shouldn't complain when they get splinters!

There is no opt out clause.

But says somebody, 'I am an atheist and I don't believe in God.' Now atheism is a very strange belief, and belief it certainly is. The atheist believes that although he has not been everywhere in the Universe and is certainly not the source of all knowledge, yet he is absolutely certain as a statement of faith that there is no God-and that is surely a massive statement of presumption. The President of America Atheist inc., once declared that 'this world would be a better place if faith was eradicated from the face of the earth.' But this misses the whole point that all atheists themselves exercise great faith in saying that there is no God. It was G.K. Chesterton who said that 'People think that when they say they don't believe in God, they believe in nothing, but the fact is that they will usually believe in anything.' However, whatever people may claim, everybody does have a god or gods that they worship. If the living God is not worshipped, then man tries to fit gods of his own making into what some have described as a 'God shaped blank in every man,' Alas, God alone fits that blank and all others don't, and to try and force them in only results in pain. Man is unique, for the Bible says that *'God created man from the dust of the earth and then breathed into him the breath of life and man became a living soul.' (Gen.2:7)* Man is not an accident. He is remarkably and wonderfully made by the Creator of the world. He is set apart and different from the rest of God's creation. Man is not a 'naked ape' as the author Desmond Morris would describe us. I have never seen a dog design a kennel, build it and then climb in it. But man is creative. He is a designer and builder, and this is not surprising because he was in the beginning made in the 'image of God' his Creator. No animals have ever been observed praying or worshipping. No animals have ever got together to start a religion that has spread around the world, or for that matter round the corner - but human beings do, as is evidenced by the multitude of religions around the world. There are not many gods and many ways, there is one God and only one way to Him, and Jesus said *'I am the way, the truth and the life, no one comes to God except by me.'(John 14:6)* If you don't accept this, your argument is not with me, it is with Jesus Himself because that is what he said of Himself The law is a court of justice, but the gospel is a throne of grace, for the law is meant to lead a sinner to faith in Christ and it does this by showing the impossibility of any other way.

But as well as coming from a society with a multiplicity of gods, the people of Israel in the Old Testament had been used to seeing on every hand material representations of these gods fashioned in wood and stone. But none of the so-called 'gods' which have been promoted throughout human history have existed outside of their inventor's imagination, and all of their exciting exploits can safely be filed away as fairy tales.

Now maybe we are not so stupid as to bow down to gods of wood and stone, the gods of the forest or the sun or the moon. Yet we do sometimes give allegiance to gods just as empty and lifeless. If you are not a worshipper of the true living God, then you have a substitute god, and to have a substitute god is to be guilty of idolatry. Jesus said, 'You shall worship the Lord your God and worship only Him.' (Matt.4:10).

So the First Commandment of the Ten leaves you in no doubt as to the position that God wants in your life. He wants the first place. We are actually totally dependent upon Him for life, and because this is so we are certainly totally responsible to Him. It is this distinctive emphasis of priority that makes the law of God so different.

There are many codes of law in human society that deal with horizontal relationships between man and his neighbour and man and the State in which he lives. But the law of God as found in the Ten Commandments has to do with a human being and his responsibility to put God first in his life.

As God's creatures made in the image of God, man is by constitution a religious creature, and revolt against God does not alter what he is by nature. His nature is to worship, and if he does not worship the one true and living God, he must needs invent a false god for the satifaction of his religiosity. Consequently, since all that is not God belongs to the realm of creation, the idolator worships an inferior creature instead of the supreme Creator. What he worships is a non-god. James Montgomery Boice the American Christian writer said that 'The universality of religion on this planet is not due to men and women being seekers after God, as some have argued. Rather, it is because they will not have God, yet need something to take God's place'

Today we pride ourselves because we no longer bow down to graven images. Idolatry, however, is by no means a thing of the past, it is just that we have become accustomed to more sophisticated, though still ancient forms of idolatry. We still find ourselves worshipping money, pleasure, the lusts of the flesh, the veneration of material possessions, luxury and the cult of worldly success, so nothing has really changed. Earl Jabey said that 'In the centre of the human heart is a throne and it is always occupied. Not a person in all the world is without a throne - and God wants to occupy the throne exclusively.'

Twentieth Century Idols

So what are some of the twentieth century idols that we in the Western World are often guilty of worshipping and putting on the throne of our lives ? The accumulation of 'things' seems to be the number one priority for so many people. Some of our modern idols are chromium plated, while others boast high performance engines and we bow down before them as we wash and polish them each Sunday morning. But maybe the universal desire to 'keep up our standard of living' has become the major idol of our time. Personal property in terms of money and clothes can equally quickly displace God in our lives. *'The love of money is the root of all evil' (1 Tim.6:10)* says the Bible. Love of money or covetousness as it might be more accurately described is very bluntly called idolatry. Paul speaks of *'Evil desires and greed which is idolatry. (Col.3:5.)* As we have more of this world's possessions we usually want more. It can then be very difficult to accurately draw a line between what are genuinely our needs and what is just being greedy. Covetousness is not only about getting riches unjustly, but in loving them inordinately, and that is the key that opens the door to many other sins. One can be covetous when you have little or much, for covetousness comes from the heart, not from the circumstances of life in which you find yourself. Much trouble comes our way when our yearnings get ahead of our earnings. Very sadly our high standard of living makes the luxuries of yesterday become the necessities of today. Trouble also comes our way when the itch of covetousness makes you scratch what you can from another man, even if it is only in your heart! The god of self often looms high on our agenda even without realising it. To love yourself nearly always leads a person to be arrogant, vain and boastful, for the self made man is a horrible example of unskilled labour. Some people make other people their gods, and we have plenty of examples of this in the extent to which some follow the stars of the pop world and sport. Hundreds of pounds are spent on being present when they perform, buying their records, wearing their colours, adulating their achievements. It is also sadly possible to make a god of our partner or even our children, if we put them first in our lives. On the gravestone of a little girl, an only child were written the words, 'Her parents put all of their wealth in this one vessel, and the shipwreck was total'. *'God says, 'No other gods before me.'* You will only meet God if you are prepared to put Him in His rightful place in your life and come to Him on His terms.

CHAPTER TWO

Prepare to Meet God

A number of years ago I was speaking in Manchester when to my great delight
a friend asked me if I would like to go and watch Manchester United play at
Old Trafford, and as you can well imagine I did not have to be asked twice.
Approaching the ground we were met by one solitary man holding up a banner
on which were written the stark words, *'Prepare to meet God'*.
You can imagine the ribald comments from some of the fans as they passed.
Maybe to be honest I felt a little embarrassed. But embarrassment turned to
shame as I reminded myself that *'Prepare to meet God'* is a very important
message in the Bible. *(Amos 4:12.)* If God is our Creator and one day we are
going to meet Him, then how important it is that we are prepared for that
meeting. So here is my blunt question, what preparation have you made to
meet God ? Death is the most democratic institution in the world. It allows
no discrimination and tolerates no exception. All that the most gifted physician
or the most brilliant surgeon can do is to postpone the inevitable. Man is
destined to die. It is our great enemy, pursuing us from infancy, disturbing
our peace and haunting our hopes, we have an appointment with death in due
course, and there are no exceptions.

In my work as a Christian speaker I visit many countries of the world and that
involves a lot of preparation. The AA Book of the road helps me plan journeys
in this country and that takes time. Other parts of the world require air tickets,
flight schedules, visas for some countries, malaria tablets, injections, phone
calls and now emails.

If you are a student you are maybe busy studying in preparation for future exams. Brides prepare for their weddings months before the actual wedding day. Some of you have already picked up holiday brochures from the travel agent to look and see where you would like to holiday next year.

At the end of the journey of life, you are not just a pile of dirt swept under the carpet, but rather you are a living soul that has to meet God your maker. Death is not the terminus, but rather the point at which you switch tracks. Woody Allen, the actor said in his rather quaint way: 'I'm not afraid of dying, I just don't want to be there when it happens.' But we all have to be there, because no one can substitute for us. Death is not a spectator sport for ever. If the nineteenth century tried to conceal the facts of life, then the twenty first century tries to conceal the fact of death.

There are some appointments that we make out of necessity. For example, a visit to the dentist because we have toothache. We don't look forward to such an appointment, but we have to keep it if we want relief from the pain. Other appointments we make and look forward too, such as a dinner date with a friend, but we do not make it because of circumstances out of our control. The car breaks down or the train is cancelled, or you are ill. But the Bible says that, *'Man is destined to die once, and after that to face judgement.'* *(Heb.9:27)* This appointment with God is already fixed, even if we do not know the date or the time. All that the Bible tells us is to make sure that we are prepared.

But what is God like ?

People often question me and say, ' You talk about God, say you believe in Him, and even claim to talk to Him in prayer, but what on earth is He like? Part of my answer to that very reasonable question is that you can discover something about Him in the Bible. *'In the beginning God'* is the first statement in the Bible, and what this is saying is that before the world came into existence, before the clock of nature was started -there was God. The universe has not always existed. The consistent teaching of the Bible is that the Cosmos had a beginning. It was not formed from any matter that already existed. God the one and only Creator of the universe, brought the world into being by the unaided power of His Word.

God is the Creator

Genesis 1:1 says, 'In the beginning God created the heavens and the earth,' and then the rest of this first chapter in the Bible goes on to outline the various stages of that wonderful creation. Isaiah the prophet writing later on in the Old Testament says that it was *'God the Lord who created the heavens, He stretched them forth, He spread out the earth.' (Isaiah 42:5).* Paul writing in the New Testament says, *'what may be known about God is plain to them, because God has made it plain to them. For since the creation of the world, God's invisible qualities -his eternal power and divine nature have been clearly seen, being understood from what has been made, so that men are without excuse.' (Rom. 1:19,20.)* It was God who flung the stars into space. It was God who set the clock of nature running and keeps it going. He continues to work in it for He is involved in the running of the universe and the forces of nature. You see, this old world of ours did not just happen, or appear by chance, or result from a big bang in the vastness of space, but rather it came into being in a direct creative act of God. Edwin Conklin the biologist said that 'the probability of life originating from accident is comparable to the possibility of the Encyclopedia Britannica resulting from an explosion in a printing press.' Our world is not the random result of a massive fluke involving matter that was always there. Creation had a beginning, and it was God who spoke it all into being. The Bible says, *'For since the creation of the world, God's invisible qualities, His eternal power and divine nature have been clearly seen.' (Rom. 1:19,20.)* Paul was of course only underlining what David had written in one of his Psalms many centuries before. *'The heavens declare the glory of God; the skies proclaim the work of his hands. Day after day they pour forth speech, night after night they display knowledge.' (Psalm 19:1,2.)*

It was Abraham Lincoln who once said, 'I find it difficult to understand why a man can look at the earth and wonder if there is a God. But I cannot understand how a person can look at the heavens and say I don't believe in God.' Professor Fred Hoyle the astronomer when asked if he thought that Darwin's theory of evolution was still plausible said, 'No -the rich assembly of plants and animals found on the earth cannot have been produced by a truism of this minor order! Any one who looks at the wonder of the universe whether through a telescope or a microscope and says that there is no God, is in the words of the Bible - a fool.

God is Spirit.

God is Spirit and that means that He has no physical dimensions, because He does not have any characteristics that we could define in terms of size and shape. He is also not confined to any one place. He is present everywhere and totally aware of all that goes on. God as the Creator of nature is not to be

identified as 'nature.' But although separate from nature He is not absent, for the Bible teaches us that He is present everywhere in the Universe. David the Psalmist says of God, *'Where can I flee from your presence ? If I go up to the heavens you are there: If l make my bed in the depths you are there. If I rise on the wings of the dawn, If I settle on the far side of the sea, even there you will guide me, your right hand will hold me fast.' (Psalm 139: 7-10).* David then goes on in the same Psalm and says *'O Lord, you have searched me and you know me. You know when I sit down: You are familiar with all my ways. Before a word is on my tongue you know it completely, O Lord.' (Psalm 139:1-4.)*
Solomon picks up the same theme in the book of Proverbs when he writes, *'The eyes of the Lord are in every place, keeping watch over the wicked and the good' (Prov.15:3).* Moving on into the New Testament we read that *'nothing in all creation is hidden from Gods sight. Everything is uncovered and laid bare before the eyes of him to whom we must give account.' (Heb.4:13.)* God not only sees men, he sees through them. It was C.S.Lewis who said, 'Do not let us deceive ourselves. No possible complexity which we can give to our picture of the Universe can hide us from God. There is no copse, no forest, no jungle thick enough to provide cover! There is never a moment of privacy from God for any one of us'. The Bible says that *'Man looks on the outward appearance, but God looks on the heart.' (I Sam. 16: 7.)*

God is Holy.

'Be holy, because I am holy,' says God in *I Peter 1:16,* for a true love for God must begin with a delight in His holiness, for when we see even a small glimpse of how holy God is, then we will bow in worship before Him. There is actually no statement in the Bible which is more demanding than the one that *'God is holy.'* This also means that He is totally committed to goodness and is always at war with evil.

Linked with God's holiness is the statement in the Bible that *'God is light and in Him there is no darkness at all.' (I John 1:5)* Reading the New Testament you discover that light and darkness are often contrasted. For example speaking of the Lord Jesus, John in his gospel says that, *'The light shines in the darkness, but the darkness has not understood it'. (John 1:5.)* Later on in the same gospel, Jesus says, *'The man who walks in the dark does not know where he is going.' (John 12:35.)* Paul writing to some Christians who lived in Ephesus warned them to beware of the *'unfruitful works of darkness.' (Eph.5:11.)* Light reveals the dirt and disorder. Light is attractive and warm, and such is the character of the God that we should prepare to meet.

God is love.

One of the most wonderful descriptions given to God is that He is love. The Bible says that *'Whoever does not love, does not know God, because God is love.'(1 John 4:8.)* This does not simply mean that God loves, although of course that is true, but rather that God is love in Himself. But of course God does love and like all true love, it is a giving, sacrificial love. John the apostle writes and says, *'This is love, not that we loved God, but that He loved us and sent His Son as an atoning sacrifice for our sins.' (1 John 4:10.)* John in his gospel tells us that, *'God so loved the world that He gave His only begotten Son, that whoever believes in Him shall not perish but have eternal life' (John 3:16.)* Jesus died on the cross not in order to make God love us, but rather because God loves us already. Calvary was the supreme demonstration of the love of God. It was C.S.Lewis who said that,' God loves us not because we are loveable but because He is love; not because He needs to receive but because He delights to give.'

God's love is of course totally undeserved in every way. The love which we have for each other is because of what we see in each other that is attractive. But God loved us when there was nothing good to be seen in us and nothing good to be said for us. John says, *'We love Him because He first loved us.' (1 John 4:19.)* God's love is infinite because God is infinite. It was F.B.Meyer who said, 'That God should pity the world I understand, because when I walk down a hospital ward and see a sick child, I pity the child. But that God should love the world -the more I think about it, the more staggered I am.'

God's love is also unchangeable. *He says in Malachi 3:6. 'I an the Lord, I change not.' In the New Testament we read that 'God does not change like shifting shadows. (James 1:17.)* Because He is also eternal then His love is eternal Since God's love had no beginning, it has no ending either, for God is from *'everlasting to everlasting.'* Joseph Hart in his well known hymn has a stanza that beautifully underlines this truth when he says,

'How good is the God we adore,
Our faithful, unchangeable friend,
His love is as great as his power,
And knows neither measure nor end.'

But maybe best of all God's love is personal. Paul said, *'It was the Son of God who loved me and gave himself for me. '(Gal.2.:20.)* This is the character of the God we need to prepare to meet.

Be prepared..

As important as this meeting will be, very tragically many people make no preparation at all. You would think that it was a non-event. Some build up a mental block to avoid thinking about it. Death is not the subject of conversation because most people think of it as something that happens to other people but not to them ! For others, any preparation is a hit and miss affair and rarely goes beyond the making of a will. Talking with a group of men one evening we got round to the subject of death and meeting with God, when one man said to me with all seriousness, 'I'll take my chance that everything will be alright.' Others have an occasional excursion towards God at Easter and Christmas, while others feel that they stand a good chance with their Maker because they live a reasonably good life and help their neighbours and the community in which they live.

But the Bible tells us that left to ourselves we are totally unprepared to meet God because we are sinners by nature and we are sinners by practice. Our sins have separated us from God, so left to ourselves we are totally unprepared to meet God. However the Bible does tell us that God has done all that is necessary in order for us to meet Him with our sin problem solved and dealt with. The Bible tells us that *'That the Father(God) sent the Son to be the Saviour of the world.' (1 John.4:14.)* On the cross when Jesus died, *'God made Him who had no sin to be sin for us, so that in Him we might become the righteousness of God ' (2 Cor.5:21.)*

The wonderful invitation of the Christian gospel is that you can 'Meet God' here and now. Meet Him as your Creator and life giver, and meet Him as your Saviour and Lord. If you meet Him as such now it will mean that when you meet Him then (at death) there will be no fear or trepidation, and certainly no judgement.. But where and how does Jesus fit into the picture and how is He relevant for today?

CHAPTER THREE
But is God For Real?

It was Karl Marx one of the founding fathers of Communism who said that 'Religion was the opium of the masses.' But was he right? Is Christianity just a sedative or is it a cure ? Is the message of the Christian gospel relevant, or is it just empty speculation ?

To the atheist, God and faith are just a fantasy of the mind, for the atheist is convinced that all religious beliefs and faith are just a delusion. Jean Paul Sartre said that 'Each human being has only himself as the sole justification for his existence. There is no ultimate objective or eternal meaning to life. An individual exists without reference to others'. The atheist believes that life with all of its complexity appeared upon the face of planet earth by a long process of evolution, therefore there is no ultimate meaning or purpose to life.

On the other hand the agnostic thinks that there is insufficient evidence to prove or disprove the existence of God and so would criticise both the atheist and the Christian for their dogmatism. Agnosticism doesn't quite deny the existence of God, but it does deny His relevance. The agnostic is a little like the actor Robert Morley who said when asked if he believed in God, 'Certainly I believe in God, but we haven't communicated lately! Or as a man said to me one night, Of course I believe in God, but I am not nuts about him as you are!'

To the humanist. God is a non-person. Swinburne echoed this when he said,

'King God is dead, glory to man in the highest, for man is the master of things.' Now if ever there was a statement of folly, this must surely be it, for man is so very far from being the master of things.

John Steinbeck won the Nobel Prize for literature several years ago. In his acceptance speech he said, 'Fearful and unprepared we have assumed Lordship over the life and death of the whole planet. So having taken God-like powers we now seek in ourselves for the responsibility and wisdom that we once prayed some deity might have.' Sadly, by saying this he was in effect throwing God overboard as being quite unnecessary in our modern world.

But experience would seem to prove the opposite of this sad philosophy. Dr. Carl Jung the Swiss psychologist said that, 'Forty years study of the human mind and emotions have given me a prescription for the sick world in which we live. Among all of my patients in the second half of life, every one of them had no faith. None were fully healed until they regained a religious outlook on life.' Could this be the reason why according to the British Medical Association, one fifth of the population of Great Britain suffer from some form of anxiety neurosis? Is this but a reflection of the fact that the majority of our population have no spiritual foundation for life ? The Bible reminds us very forcibly that *'what is seen is temporary, but what is unseen is eternal.' (2 Cor.4:18.)* Surprisingly it was Albert Einstein who wrote to a friend shortly before he died and said that, 'The need of the world is to restore God to the centre of its thinking.'

Has God left us in the dark?

Now just suppose for the sake of argument that as a Christian I am right, and there is a God, and that recognising my inability to communicate with Him, He took the initiative and came looking for me. Then of course the next question, has He ever done so ? And the claim of the Christian gospel is that God has done precisely that. God has not left us in the dark. He has switched on the light, because when Jesus came just over 2000 years ago, God came. He came into human history in the person of Jesus Christ, and this is a major foundation stone of the Christian faith.. Listen to what the Bible says in John's Gospel chapter 1. *'In the beginning was the Word, and the Word was with God and the Word was God. The Word was made flesh and made his dwelling among us.' (John 1:1,2, 14.)*

The incarnation of Jesus Christ was a necessary means to an end, and the end was the putting away of the sin of the world by His death on the cross. The glory of the incarnation is that it presents to our gaze not a humanized God or a deified man, but a true God-man; one who is all that God is, and at the same time all that man is. He is the one whose almighty arm we can rest on, and to whose human sympathy we can appeal to, for if you meet Jesus Christ, you will meet God.

Now all of the great religious leaders of the world have usually been asked from time to time who they were and Jesus was no exception, and there were three very important things that Jesus had to say or do in answering that question.

First of all...

He very clearly and dogmatically said that He was God. *'Show us God'* was the challenge put to Him on one occasion, and he replied *'If you have seen me, you have seen God.'* Once in his earthly ministry Jesus said, *'Before Abraham was, I am (using the title of God.) At this they picked up stones to stone him, but Jesus hid himself; slipping away from the temple grounds. (John 8:59)*

Now although a mentally disturbed person might claim to be God, usually their behaviour would indicate their disturbed state of mind. None of the leaders or founders of the major world religions ever made such claims. They may have claimed to have divine authority, or to having received a revelation from God, or even to say that they were prophets sent by God, but none have ever made such a claim to deity as Jesus did.

Muhammad, the founder of the Islamic faith, wholeheartedly worked day and night to found his new religion, but he never claimed deity. Sometimes his followers tried to worship him and he always rebuked them for their folly. In fact in the Koran, the Holy Book of Islam, Muhammad says to his people that he is 'only mortal like them.' In fact the single unpardonable sin in Islam is to lay claim to deity.

Buddha as he approached the end of his life was asked how he wished to be remembered. In replying he urged his followers not to worry about remembering him, the essential thing was to remember his teaching. But Jesus was quite the opposite. When he instituted the communion service he said, *'Do this in remembrance of me.'* There is no question as you read the gospel but that Jesus claimed to be God revealed in human flesh

It was C.S.Lewis who said 'A man who was merely a man and said the sort of things that Jesus said wouldn't be a great moral teacher. He'd either be a lunatic - on a level with a man who says he's a poached egg or else he would be the devil of hell. You must make your choice. Either this man was and is the Son of God, or else a madman or something worse...But don't let us come up with any patronizing nonsense about his being a great human teacher. He hasn't left that open to us. He didn't intend to.'

Secondly..

Jesus acted as we would expect God to act. He showed His mastery over every type of disease, from congenital to contagious.. He was the Master of natural law. He changed water into wine in a moment; a process which in God's arrangement of nature normally speaking takes months. He walked on the water because He was not bound by the laws of gravity. He even raised the dead on at least three occasions.

But there is an interesting story in Mark 2 that illustrates in a powerful way his deity. It is the story of the paralytic in Capernaum. Some friends brought a man lying on a bed to the house where Jesus was staying. But it was impossible to get in, so they climbed up onto the roof, made an opening and lowered the man down at the feet of Jesus. The words of Jesus to the man were startling, for he said, *'Son, your sins are forgiven'*. The response of the Jewish leaders was immediate and direct and the Bible says that *'they were thinking in their hearts, who can forgive sin but God alone.'* They were of course absolutely right in what they thought, for only God can forgive sin, because all sin is against God. They certainly were not meaning to bear witness to the claims of Christ, but that is just what they were unconsciously doing. The reply of Jesus was electrifying, for He said, *'Which is easier, to say to the paralytic, your sins are forgiven, or to say, get up, take your mat and walk. But that you may know that the Son of Man has authority on earth to forgive sins he said to the paralytic, I tell you get up, take your mat and go home.'(Matthew 2:1-11)* - and up he got and home he went !" His claim to be God and therefore able to forgive sin was demonstrated by this physical miracle. It was C.S.Lewis in commenting on this miracle who said,' Now it is quite understandable for a man to forgive something you do to him. But what on earth would you say, if somebody had done you out of £20 and I said, "that's all right, I forgive him !" But that is precisely what Jesus said.' There is no question but that Jesus acted as if He were God The characteristics of God Almighty are mirrored for us in Jesus Christ. Therefore if we want to know what God is like we must study the life of Jesus Christ. Again let me quote from C.S.Lewis who said, 'Christians believe that Jesus Christ is the Son of God because He said so, and the other evidence about Him has convinced them that He was neither a lunatic nor a quack.

Thirdly..

Jesus said that He had come on a rescue mission from God. Before He was born an angel appeared to Joseph and not only told him the good news about the Virgin conception of Mary, but also told him that *'she will give birth to a son, and you are to give him the name Jesus, because he will save his people from their sin.' (Matt. 1:21.)*

Joseph was not only told the sex of the baby that Mary was carrying, but also the name he was to be given. Shepherds in the fields surrounding Bethlehem were also told by angels who this Jesus was. *'The angel said to them, do not be afraid, I bring you good news of great joy that will be for all the people. Today in the town of David a Saviour has been born to you; He is Christ the Lord.' (Luke 2:10,11.)* There is no question but that Jesus came to be a Saviour, a rescuer, a deliverer. But the question that follows must surely be, why was he needed, what do we need saving from ? The answer is surely found in what the New Testament goes on to explain. *'Here is a trustworthy saying that deserves full acceptance; Christ Jesus came into the world to save sinners.' (1 Tim.2:15.)*

Audience response.

Some of those who listened to His remarkable claims were consumed by rage, and even on one occasion took up stones to stone Him. Others however were totally convinced that He was who He said He was. Thomas one of his first disciples could not accept the resurrection of Jesus at first. But when Jesus appeared to him he was convinced and said, *'My Lord and my God' (John 20:28.)* He has been followed since by countless thousands who have discovered that faith is not a fantasy but rather a life transforming experience - because in meeting up with Jesus they have met up with God.

CHAPTER FOUR

Meet God as You Face the Claims of Christ

On one busy day in the life of Jesus He had spent a lot of time answering questions. But now he turns the tables and asks the people one simple question. *'What do you think about the Christ?' (Matt.22:42.)* Although it was the first time that He had put the question in words, it was really a question that He posed every day of His life. Because His person was unique and different, along with His claims and message, they always posed a challenge. As the infamous musical, 'Jesus Christ Superstar' puts it, 'Do you think you are who they say you are?'

Now there is an interesting phrase in the gospels that says of Jesus, *'there was a division amongst the people because of him,'(John 7:43.)* and if it was true then, it is equally true today. Jesus himself put it so clearly when he said, *'If you are not for me, you are against me.'(Matt. 12:30.)*

But why did Jesus divide?

Basically for two reasons. First of all because He claimed to be God revealed in human flesh. Secondly, because of what He claimed to be able to give to people in terms of pardon and forgiveness. His claims were so unique, repeated and enlarged upon, that they were impossible of misunderstanding. Christianity is either a total fabrication or else it is true. If it is true and Jesus Christ is the Son of God, the Saviour of the world, then we ought to listen to what he has to say.

Doubting Thomas as he so often is (I think unfairly) called, asked Jesus, *'How can we know the way?'*, and Jesus replied, *'I am the way, the truth and*

the life, no one comes to the Father except through me.' (John 14:6) Later on the same day Jesus was asked, *'Lord show us the Father and that will be enough for us.* Jesus in replying spelt out very clearly who He was when he said, *'anyone who has seen me has seen the Father,' (John 14:9)*
So what do you think about the Christ ? Is he true or false ? But before you give your verdict, let me bring before you other witnesses, because God never calls us to blind faith. Christian faith is faith based upon reasonable evidence.

There are other Witnesses

Our first witness is a book, and that is the witness of the Old Testament. Jesus called for its witness to His person and claims when he challenged the Jewish leaders and said, *'These are the Scriptures that testify about me.' (John 1:39)*
He was of course referring to the Old Testament that the Jews had preserved and revered from the time of Moses. One of the remarkable things about the Old Testament is the multitude of prophecies concerning the birth, life, death and resurrection of Jesus Christ. All of them written centuries before and all of them without exception accurately fulfilled. There was no way that he could possibly have arranged to fit in with them all as some agnostics have suggested.

Let me give you just one of these 500 plus prophecies about him. In the Old Testament in Isaiah 7:14 written over five centuries before his birth the prophet wrote, *'Therefore the Lord himself will give you a sign: The virgin will be with child and will give birth to a son and will call him Immanuel.'* Turning to the Gospel of Matthew, the angel of the Lord spoke to Joseph and said, *"Joseph son of David, do not be afraid to take Mary home as your wife, because what is conceived in her is from the Holy Spirit. She will give birth to a son, and you are to give him the name Jesus, because he will save his people from their sins". All this took place to fulfil what the Lord had said through the prophet. "The virgin will be with child and will give birth to a son, and they will call him Immanuel" which means "God with us". (Matt. 1:22, 23.)*

Our second witness to consider is the testimony of what Jesus did in terms of the miraculous. *'Believe me,'* said Jesus, *'when I say that I am in the Father and the Father in me: or at least believe on the evidence of the miracles themselves.' (John 14:11)* None of the miracles of Jesus were haphazard demonstrations of power or magic, they were all associated with claims that he made. There were plenty of eyewitnesses to what happened apart from those who actually experienced them in their lives. On one occasion in the ministry of Jesus He rebuked the city of Capernaum, a city in which he had performed many miracles and said to them *'If the miracles that were performed in you had been performed in Sodom, it would have remained to this day. But I tell you that it will be more bearable for Sodom on the day of judgement than for you.'* *(Matt.ll:23,24.)*

The third witness is the Holy Spirit. Before Jesus went back to Heaven he told his disciples that when he had gone he would send the Holy Spirit to them and *'When the Counsellor (the Holy Spirit) comes whom I will send to you from the Father, he will testify about me.' (John 16:26.)* On the Day of Pentecost, that promise of Jesus was fulfilled, and those fearful trembling first disciples were remarkably transformed. Following that remarkable event, wherever they went they preached the message of the forgiveness of sins in Jesus Christ. Many others believed this message, not because of the oratory or forceful presentation of the apostles, but because the Holy Spirit was witnessing in their hearts that Jesus was indeed the Son of God, the Saviour of the World

But the fourth witness is surely a remarkable ongoing one and that is the testimony of individual men and women from all walks of life who have found Christ to be who He said He was. All over the world you can meet people from different nations and cultures who will tell you that they met God when they met Jesus Christ and received him into the their lives, and surely that must mean something ?

So ladies and gentlemen of the jury, what is your verdict. Is Jesus Christ true or false. Is he an impostor, or is He who He said he was. What do you think of Christ ?

But moving on in the gospel narrative of the New Testament, another question looms on the horizon. It comes during the trial and miscarriage of justice when Jesus was hauled up in front of Pilate by the Jewish authorities. After examining Him he brought Him out in front of the crowd and said, *'What shall I do with Jesus who is called the Christ?' (Matt.27:22.)* History sadly records what he did, and the name of Pilate is always associated with cowardice and shame. So the question that you need to face is that, if you have come to have right thoughts about Jesus, then, what will you do with Jesus who is called the Christ ?

People make different responses.

Some exclude Him from their lives because of their sin. One of the Huxley brothers was once asked why he did not believe in Christ, and he replied, 'I have reasons for not believing because I recognise that believing brings with it moral obligations, and these I do not want to face.' Jesus underlined this rebellious streak in human nature when he said, *'This is the verdict: Light has come into the world, but men loved darkness instead of light because their deeds were evil.' (John 3:19.)*

One evening as darkness descended upon his town Robert Louis Stevenson stood as a boy at the window of his home and watched the darkness cover the street outside. 'Come and sit down,' called his mother, you can't see anything out there.' But young Stevenson insisted that he could. 'I can see something wonderful,' he told his mother. 'There is a man coming up the street making holes in the darkness.' It was the lamplighter ! And Jesus Himself, as the Light of the world is the only one who can punch holes in the darkness of sin, but sadly so many people do not want His light to shine into their dark hearts.

Other people make all kinds of excuses as to why they do not come to Christ and become Christians. The inconsistencies of professing Christians is a problem for some. Others try to evade the issue and build up a mental block to shut God out of their thinking. But we all need to be reminded that no human being can escape God for ever. The Bible says quite clearly, *'It is appointed unto man once to die and after death the judgment.' (Heb.9:27.)* Dr. Wilber Penfield the Director of the Montreal Neurological Institute said in a report to the Smithsonian Institute, 'Your brain contains a permanent record of your past that is like a single continuous strip of movie film, complete with sound tract. This 'film library' records your whole waking life from childhood on. You can live again those scenes from your past, one at a time, when a surgeon applies a gentle electrical current to a certain point on the temporal cortex of your brain.' The report goes on to say that as you relive the scene from your past, you feel exactly the same emotions that you did during the original experience. Could it be that the human race will be confronted by this irrefutable record at the judgement bar of God when as Paul says in *Romans 2:16. 'God will judge men's secrets through Jesus Christ, as my gospel declares.'*

But you can find forgiveness.

One of the great barriers between you and God according to the Bible is your sin. It is only when that barrier is removed and you know God's forgiveness that you can meet God without fear. But how can you find forgiveness ? One of the first great preachers of the Christian faith was the apostle Paul, and on one occasion when in the city of Pisidian Antioch he went into the Synagogue on the Sabbath day and made a bold declaration about God's forgiveness and how to obtain it. He said, *'I want you to know that through Jesus, the forgiveness of sins is proclaimed to you.' (Acts 13:38.)* It was Frank Retief of South Africa who said 'We cannot experience God's forgiveness until our sins have been dealt with.' And thank God Jesus dealt with them at the cross.

There are of course many ways in which people search for forgiveness, and world religions testify to man's unending quest for this assurance. Here in our Western World, many try to find forgiveness in going faithfully through the rites of their church. Others feel that in giving themselves to good works and upright living that they will find forgiveness. But the Bible quite clearly says that it is, *'By grace you are saved through faith, and not of yourselves.' (Eph. 2:5)*

It was of course 'Jesus the forgiver of sins' that the shepherds of Bethlehem were told about that first Christmas, when the angelic visitors declared to them that *'unto you is born this day in the City of David a Saviour who is Christ the Lord.' (Luke 2:10.)*

But if his birth was remarkable, his life was outstanding. As a youth we are told that, *'He increased in wisdom and stature and in favour with God and man.' (Luke 2:52.)* It was said of him by those who listened to his teaching that *'No one ever spoke the way this man does.' (John 7:46.)* He was the healer and miracle worker, and his life was totally devoted to others. He was without fault and he radiated joy, peace and love. Jesus could turn to the religious leaders of his day and say, *'Can any of you' prove me guilty of sin.' (John 8:46.)* - and none could. His life was outstanding in every way, and what a challenge that presents to us today.

So what reason did they have for killing Him ? The testimony of all was that He was faultless, for the Jewish authorities had to hire false witnesses to testify against Him. Pilate the Roman Judge said, *'I find no basis for a charge against this man.' (Luke 23:4)* Judas after the betrayal cried out *'I have betrayed innocent blood.' (Matt 27:24.)* The thief being crucified beside him said, *'This man has done nothing wrong.' (Luke 23:41.)* Even the Roman Centurion responsible for the execution said, *'Surely this was a righteous man.' (Luke 23:47.)*

By birth, life and deeds, he was perfectly holy, yet in *Luke 23:24* we read. *'But with loud shouts they insistently demanded that he be crucified, and their shouts prevailed. So Pilate decided to grant their demands: He released the man who had been asked for, and surrendered Jesus to their will.'*

What followed next was the greatest judicial murder in history. The one who bathed his disciples feet and laid his hands on little children was given nails for his hands and feet. The one whose brow was wreathed with smiles was given a thorny crown to wear. The one who said, *'If any one is thirsty let him come to me and drink.' (John 7:37),* said on the cross, *'I thirst.' (John l 19:28.)* And the one who promised his disciples of all generations *'Never will I leave you, never will I forsake you.'(Heb 13:51)* cried out on the cross *'My God, my God, why have you forsaken me.' (1Matt 27:46.)*

But this was no stroke of fate, this was no tragic accident of history. After the crucifixion and then the resurrection He appeared to his disciples on numerous occasions. At one of these appearances we are told *'he opened their minds so they could understand the Scriptures. This is what is written: the Christ will suffer and rise from the dead on the third day, and repentance and forgiveness of sins will be preached in his name to all nations.' (Luke 24:45-47.)*

This man, the God man, by his death on the cross for our sins was making a way for the barrier to be removed and for God to be able to freely forgive. In the Old Testament in the book of Isaiah, God describes in a vivid way what he has done for us in Christ. *'We all like sheep have gone astray, each of us has turned to his own way, and the Lord has laid on him the iniquity of us all.' (Isaiah 53:6)* Coming into the New Testament for an explanation the apostle Peter says, *'For Christ died for our sins once for all, the righteous for the unrighteous to bring us to God'.(I Peter 1:18)* And the Bible says that *'when they had carried out all that was written about him, they took him down from the tree, and laid him in a tomb.' (Acts 13:29.)*

Humanly speaking He was finished. His mission had failed. There was a huge stone and a Roman guard making sure that he stayed in that tomb. But listen, *'God raised him from the dead.' (Acts 4:10.)* It is because Christ is alive that Paul could declare, *'I want you to know that through Jesus the forgiveness of sin is proclaimed to you.' Acts 13:38,39.*

The Resurrection changed everything.

His resurrection was no hallucination as some critics would suggest. Old Testament prophets who wrote of his death also wrote of his resurrection. David the Psalmist wrote, *'You will not abandon me to the grave, nor will you let your Holy One see decay.' (Psalm 16:10)* Jesus promised it right at the beginning of his ministry. *"Then the Jews demanded of him, 'What miraculous signs can you show us to prove your authority to do all this?'"* Jesus answered them, *'Destroy this temple, and I will raise it again,'* The Jews replied. *'It has taken forty-six years to build this temple and you are going to raise it in three days ? But the temple he had spoken of was his body. (John 2:18-20*

After His resurrection He appeared to Mary Magdalene, to the two women at the tomb, to the apostles when Thomas was absent, and then again when he was present. He appeared to the disciples- by the Sea of Tiberias and on the road to Emmaus. He also appeared to a crowd of 500. Last of all says Paul, *'The Lord appeared to me' (1 Cor. 15).* The last thing that we read about Jesus is that *'while He was blessing them, He left them and was taken up into heaven' (Luke 24:51)*

If Jesus had stayed in the tomb, there would be no salvation for you and me, and there certainly would be not forgiveness of sins. Because God raised Jesus from the dead, He was declaring that the sacrifice of Christ on the cross was sufficient. It is now through the crucified, risen and now living Saviour that you can at this very moment receive the forgiveness of sins. It was Donald Grey Barnhouse who said, 'the resurrection of Christ is our receipted bill of acceptance. The Easter story ends not with a funeral but with a festival.'

What was it that turned these shivering, frightened men into men that turned the world upside down ? It was the indisputable fact that Christ had risen from the dead. Men who at one time fled in fear, now stood and fearlessly preached this fact. Paul writing a letter to Christians who lived in Corinth said, *'And if Christ has not been raised, our preaching is useless and so is your faith, you are yet in your sins.' (1 Cor.15:14.)* But Christ is risen and there is salvation and forgiveness. *'I want you to know,'* says Paul, *'that through Jesus, the forgiveness of sins is proclaimed to you.' (Acts 13:38.)* Only forgiven sinners meet God without fear. But God has not promised to forgive a single sin that man is not willing to forsake.

Isaiah writing in the Old Testament says, *'Seek the Lord while he may be found, call on him while he is near. Let the wicked forsake his way and the evil man his thoughts. Let him turn to the Lord and He will have mercy on him, and to our God for he will abundantly pardon.' (Isaiah 55:6, 7.)*

So how are you facing up to the challenge of Christ, that you can meet God and find forgiveness and newness of life in Him? It was Napoleon who said, 'Ages roll by, nations die and nations rise and fall and others take their place.

Civilisations crumble and new eras dawn, but to the end of time it will be seen that the figure of Jesus Christ stands above all.' But although he does stand above all, yet He is near and you can discover Him, for He is as near as the breath you breathe.

CHAPTER FIVE

Meet God as You Face the Challenge of Christ

I remember a few years ago sitting in the ruins of the old city of Capernaum and turning over the pages of my New Testament and reading yet again some of the many things that Jesus did in Galilee. It was in Cana of Galilee that he performed his first miracle when he turned water into wine. On a nearby hillside he fed 5000, and then down in the Synagogue he delivered a demon possessed man. Peter's mother-in-law was healed in this city and Matthew the tax collector was called by Jesus to follow Him, and we are told that as a result he left all and followed Jesus. A Roman Centurion's servant was healed there. You would have thought that with all that had happened in Capernaum unbelief would have been impossible, or at least inexcusable. Crowds followed Him in Galilee, and for a brief season he was their popular hero.

Yet, to be honest, very few of them gave any sign that their consciences were stirred or that they had truly repented. Jesus had challenged them concerning his claims to be the Bread of Life. He had told them, *'I am the living bread that came down from Heaven. If a man eats of this bread, he will live for ever. This bread is my flesh, which I will give for the life of the world. I tell you the truth, unless you eat the flesh of the Son of Man and drink his blood, you have no life in you.' (John 6: 51;53.)* Now of course Jesus was not meaning this literally, but he was teaching that his life, his blood, his death, and his resurrection were going to be the means whereby they could meet God and be right with Him. But the response of these people so challenged by Jesus was, *'This is a hard saying, who can accept it.' (John 6:60)* You see, it wasn't the miracles that challenged them. What really challenged them was the teaching of Jesus and the claims that he was making upon their lives.

So what kind of disciples were they?

Notice that these people are described as *'his disciples.' (John 6:61.)* But they obviously were not the twelve, for Jesus turns to the twelve and says, *'Do you want to leave as well.' (John 6:67.)* No, these so called disciples were just hangers on. They possibly had been part of the 5000 who had been fed on the hillside by the lake. They were after the spectacular and could not handle the real issues of what it meant to follow after Christ. They wanted to meet God on their terms, and it was not possible then or now.

Sadly there are those today who believe that if we could see mighty signs and wonders people would believe. If the deaf could hear and the lame could walk. If people could have their teeth filled with gold as some would claim, then non Christians would believe in Christ. But it wasn't true in the days of Jesus and it is not true today, for sadly, seeing is not believing.

So what was this 'hard teaching' that they could not face? The word 'hard' used here is an interesting word. It means 'rough and harsh.' What Jesus said and taught was not difficult to understand, but it was challenging to accept. Their problem was not in their minds, it was in their hearts. You see, it was not that these people of Capernaum found the language of Christ so obscure as to be unintelligible, but rather it was what he said that was irreconcilable with their own views. Jesus was aware that these disciples were grumbling and he turned to them and said, *'Does this offend you.' (John 6:61.)* Jesus made discipleship hard and so lost many prospective followers, the reason being that he called them and us to a pilgrimage and not a parade, to a fight and not just a frolic.

So they were offended by Jesus.

Now as we look at this particular situation at the end of John chapter 6 there appears to have been five things that offended these so called followers of Jesus Christ. They were first of all offended by the statement of Jesus that he was going to give his body and his blood so that people might be forgiven by God and find salvation. This truth proclaimed today often produces the same reaction.. 'this is a hard saying.' Christianity is accused of being a religion of blood. And in one sense it is. The shedding of the blood of Christ on the cross for our sin is on the surface repulsive. It speaks of the shame and death of the Lord Jesus Christ. But it also represents salvation and deliverance from sin and its awful guilt, and in this sense the cross is the most attractive symbol in the world. Peter in his first epistle writes, *'For you know that it was not with perishable things such as silver and gold that you were redeemed from the empty way of life handed down to you from your forefathers, but with the precious blood of Christ, a lamb without blemish or defect.' (1 Peter 1:18-19.)* Peter follows this up in the next chapter of his letter and says, *'He himself bore our sins in his body on the cross.' (1 Peter 2:23.)* It was Martin Luther who said that Jesus Christ never died for our good works, they were not worth dying for. But he gave himself for our sins, according to the Scriptures.'

Secondly, Jesus made another fascinating claim. He said. *'What if you see the Son of Man ascend to where he was before'! (John 6:62.)* So what was He getting at ? He first of all speaks of himself as the Son of Man, and of course He was truly human, but He also said that he would ascend to where he was before. In saying this he was by implication declaring his resurrection, because he says that he was going back to where He had come from. Here was surely an implied claim to deity. He was the Son of Man, but He was also the Son of God.

Paul later on writing in the New Testament said of Jesus, *'And being found in appearance as a man, he humbled himself and became obedient to death - even death on a cross. Therefore God exalted him to the highest place and gave him the name that is above every name, that at the name of Jesus, every knee should bow, in heaven and on earth, and every tongue confess that Jesus Christ is Lord to the glory of God the Father.' (Phil.2:8-11.)* Does this claim of Jesus offend you?

Thirdly, Jesus said, *'The Spirit gives life; the flesh counts for nothing. The words I have spoken unto you are spirit and they are life.'(John6:63.)* And what Jesus was saying here is that the flesh, the natural man, is of zero value in terms of being able to make a person alive to God. The natural man has no part in the work of salvation. It is not 'Something in my hand I bring and to your cross I also cling.' Rather it is in the words of the old hymn, 'Nothing in my hand I bring and to your cross alone I cling.' Paul reminds us, *'it is by grace you have been saved through faith and this not from yourselves, it is the gift of God, nor by works so that no one can boast.'(Ephesians 2:8)* Grace is the free, unearned favour of God towards us sinners, and only made possible because of the death of Jesus on the cross. It is a free gift to be received by faith alone and not because of something that you are or do.

Salvation is not produced by the logical argument of the mind, or any hypnotic power brought to bear upon the will. Nor is it produced by a touching appeal to the emotions, or beautiful music or hearty singing, nor even the skill of the preacher. It is the Holy Spirit who quickens. Jesus said that 'The words I have spoken unto you are spirit and they are life.' (John 6:33.) Only the Holy Spirit can quicken a man or woman and make them come alive to God. When a person receives the words of Christ into their heart and life, then and only then do they begin to live. Jesus said, *'I have come that they might have life and have it more abundantly.'(John 10.10.)* For you see, although the Holy Spirit is the divine agent, the Word of God is the divine instrument, for Jesus said *'The words I have spoken to you are Spirit and they are life.'(John 6:63.)* James tell us that *'He chose to give us birth through the word of truth.'(James 1:18.)* Peter repeated this truth when he wrote, *'For you have been born again, not of perishable seed, but of imperishable, through the living and enduring word of God.' (1 Peter 1:23.)*

So notice the divine balance. God's Holy Spirit quickens and convicts an individual, for Jesus said that *'the Spirit gives life, the flesh counts for nothing'. (John 6:63)* But we also need to take heed to obey God's Word, for, *'God commands all men everywhere to repent.'(Acts 17:30)* So does this command offend you ?

Fourthly, Jesus said, *'Yet there are some of you who do not believe.'(John 6:61.)*, and unbelief is also a characteristic of many contemporary people in our world today. But Jesus has warned us that *'If you believe not that I am he you will die in your sins.'(John 8:23.)* Then the writer to the Hebrews in the New Testament reminds us that, *'We must pay more careful attention therefore to what we have heard, so that we do not drift away. For if the message spoke by angels was binding, and violation and disobedience received its just punishment, how shall we escape if we neglect such a great salvation.' (Heb.2:1,2)* Hearing always brings a responsibility to respond.

Jesus then went on to challenge these people in Capernaum, for he was not deceived by outward appearances. They might be posing as his disciples, they might even seem to be very devoted to him, but he knew that they had not believed. They did not accept his words, therefore they did not have the Spirit of God abiding in them, nor did they have life.

Fifthly, they were offended because Jesus had said, *'No one can come to me, unless the Father who sent me draws him,' (John 6:43.)* We do not save ourselves, and will you notice that Jesus said, *'No one can come,'* It is not a question of would not come,' but 'cannot come.' You see the will of the natural man has nothing to do with it. John speaks of Christians as *'children born not of natural descent, nor of human decision or a husband's will, but born of God'(John 1:13.)* Paul writing to Timothy says that *'God has saved us and called us, not because of anything we have done but because of his own purpose and grace.'(2 Tim. 1:9)* No sinner is ever saved by giving his heart to God. We are not saved by our giving, we are saved by God's giving. So does this offend you ?

So facing this five fold challenge, John tells us that *'From this time, many of his disciples turned back and no longer followed him.'(John 6:66)* These so called disciples were fringe followers, and the cost of genuine discipleship was too great for them. Jesus was claiming to be Lord, and to accept this meant submitting to his authority. Jesus claimed total allegiance and self denial, and they could not face this challenge and demand., for Jesus will not be a Saviour to anyone who refuses to bow to him as Lord.

But there were the real disciples.

Jesus now turns to speak to the twelve and says, *'You do not want to leave, do you'?* Or as the A.V. puts it, *'Will you also go away?'* The immediate reply of Peter was illuminating. *'Lord to whom shall we go? You have the words of eternal life.'(John 6:68,69.)* Peter was speaking personally, but he was also speaking for all of the disciples. Notice how he addresses Jesus as Lord, and he uses this title in its fullest meaning. In *verse 63* Jesus had spoken of himself as the *'Son of Man.'* and of course Peter knew that this was true. But he also recognised and testified to the deity of Jesus and called him Lord.

Miracles, signs and wonders had attracted the crowds, but the teaching and claims of Christ had repelled them. But it was the opposite for Peter. It was not the supernatural works but the divine words of the Lord Jesus which held him. Peter had what the *'many disciples who went back.'* did not have - the hearing ear. Jesus had said in *verse 63. 'The words I have spoken unto you are spirit and they are life.'* Peter's testimony of affirmation to Jesus were, *'You have the words of eternal life.'* The words of Jesus had sunk deep into his soul. He had felt their power. He was conscious of the blessings that they had imparted to him. *'For faith comes from hearing the message, and the message is heard through the word of Christ.' (Rom. 10:17.)*

Following this initial question of *'Lord to whom shall we go, you have the words of eternal life.'* Peter makes a great declaration of faith as he says, *'We believe·and know that you are the Holy One of God.' (John 6:69.)* Note the order of the words of Peter, *'We believe and know.'* But whoever heard of believing in order to know ?

Naturally speaking we might think that it ought to be the other way round. In other words, once we know, then we can believe ! But Peter had grasped the divinely appointed way, for God's thoughts are not our thoughts, for faith must come first. The natural man says, show it to me, prove it. seeing is believing. But God reverses the order of things. The writer of the book of Hebrews says, *'By faith we understand that the Universe was formed at God's command so that what is seen was not made out of what was visible.' (Heb. 11:13.)* It is only through faith that we understand any part of God's Word. We believe and are sure. God then rewards our faith by giving us an assurance as far as spiritual things are concerned. The A.V. puts Peter's reply in this way, *'And we believe and know that you are the Holy One of God. '(John 6:69.)*

Peter knew by now that there was nobody else that he could turn to. He knew something of the empty, cold, religious formalism of the Pharisees and the Sadducees. He certainly had observed the materialism and social life of the Romans and the Greeks, and he knew that none of this could satisfy the soul of man and he turned to Jesus and said, *'You have the words of life.'* Jesus and Jesus alone has the answers. He has the social answer, the political answer, and above all he has the personal answer. Jesus has the answer to your biggest problem, the problem of your sin. It is sin that causes war and unrest in the world. It is sin that is ruining our world, society and also the lives of men and women. Sin is failure, ungodliness, lawlessness, unrighteousness, impurity, selfishness and deceit. Sin separates us from God. It is transgression of God's laws. It is the omission of good. It is unbelief. Sin is an affront to God's holiness, and sin will eventually shut you out of heaven unless you are forgiven. The problem of sin is your problem and mine, and Jesus is God's answer to our sin problem. Get the sin question settled and you will meet God. But how is the sin question dealt with ? Our next chapter will let you into the secret.

CHAPTER SIX

But You Can Only Meet God at the Cross

Most people would recognise the cross as the international symbol of the Christian faith, and whether it is in the form of beautiful jewellery or the stark concrete or marble cross in a cemetery, it speaks of the person of Jesus Christ. But it also speaks of the manner of his death by crucifixion, and it is in the pages of the New Testament that we get the answer to the question, 'But why did he die ?'

Great figures in human history have had books written about their lives, deeds and words, and then merely as an afterthought it says that on such and such a day they died. But the death of Jesus Christ is majored on in all of the New Testament books. It was Alexander MacLaren who said, 'the cross is the centre of the world's history. The incarnation of Christ and the crucifixion of Jesus are the pivot round which all the events of the ages revolve.' Paul the great preacher and writer of the early Christian church made some startling statements during his ministry, but possibly none more startling than when he wrote, *'May I never boast except in the cross of our Lord Jesus Christ.'(Gal 6:14.)*

But we must resist the temptation to sentimentalise the cross. To change it into a jewelled ornament is not to enhance it, it is rather to obscure its meaning. The cross is a gibbet, the gruesome instrument of the most shameful of deaths. Properly understood it should convince us of the enormity of our sin and of the infinite cost to God of our redemption. It is an object as ghastly as our sin is foul. It is defiling and dishonouring to God.

So what on earth was there for Paul to boast about or glory in as far as the cross and the death of Christ was concerned? The cross was the ultimate demonstration of the rejection of all that was good and pure and truthful. It was such a perversion of justice that even nature itself trembled, for as Jesus was crucified, darkness descended upon the earth. But Paul did glory in the cross, for the cross was but the darkness before the dawn. Calvary and Easter were but one day apart.

Friedriche Nietzsche said that the 'cross was a symbol of weakness, unworthy of a real man.' In his defiance of God he went mad. But in the last days of his life he was cared for by a Christian nurse. Significantly and yet tragically, he who rejected the crucified Saviour signed one of his last letters as from the 'Crucified.' Man cannot escape from the cross.

At the cross, in the death of Christ, God was making a way of reconciliation for us with Himself, for the Bible says that *'God was reconciling the world to himself in Christ, not counting men's sins against them.' (2 Cor.5.:18.)* When we talk about reconciliation we are talking about bringing into a friendly relationship two parties who are at variance with each other, and removing that which caused the estrangement in the first place.

Our sins had brought about our separation from God, for the Bible says *'But your iniquities have separated you from your God, your sins have hidden his face from you.'(Isaiah 59:2)* It is the problem of the religious and the atheist, the educated and the uneducated, the rich and the poor, and it is your problem as well.

God's laws are not set up by finding out what most people do and then calling it normal. God's laws are in keeping with God's character and they are absolute and holy. Sin is missing the mark, but it is also the omission of good. It starts in the heart, for the Bible says that, *'Out of the overflow of the heart the mouth speaks. The good man brings things out of the good stored up in him, and the evil man brings evil things out of the evil stored up in him.' (Matt. 12:34, 35.)* But it can also be just plain unbelief, for Jesus said, *'If you believe not that I am He you will die in your sin'.* Sin separates us from God and so we need reconciliation, and the death of Christ on the cross declares the wonderful possibility and provision for us to be reconciled to God. In addition, the death of Christ on the cross brings to us a righteousness from God that we do not naturally have nor can achieve. God because of His character cannot overlook our sin. He must always punish sin and deal with it. At the cross,

God the righteous judge stepped from the judgement throne and in the person of Christ took our punishment. Paul writing about this awesome event says, *'For He has made him to be sin for us, who knew no sin, that we might be made the righteousness of God in Him.' (2Cor.5:21.)*

Following on from this tremendous event, he goes on to say, *'Now to him that worketh not, bur believeth on him that justifieth the ungodly, his faith is counted for righteousness.' (Rom. 4:5.)* Repenting of your sin and trusting Christ as your Saviour and Lord of your life means that God will accept you and count you as righteous in His sight.

But lastly, the death of Christ is the doorway to new life in Christ. Jesus not only died on the cross for our sins, He rose again from the dead and is now the living Lord who can enter our lives and change and transform us. The Bible says of such a person that, *'Therefore if anyone is in Christ he is a new creation, the old has gone and the new has come.'(2 Cor.5:17.)* You can meet God because of the cross. It was St. Augustine who said, 'The cross is the pulpit from which Christ preached God's love to the world.' There is no question but that the cross loudly proclaims God's hatred of man's sin, but equally it magnificently declares God's love for sinners like you and me, and his great desire that we might be saved from our sin, its penalty and its bondage. So what should be our response to the cross, its meaning and application in our lives ? As we shall see in the next chapter it is a call to face our sin and repent of it. But what does it mean to repent?

CHAPTER SEVEN

Meet God in Repentance

We live today in a world full of voices, all of them clamouring for our attention. There are the voices of world statesmen, politicians, scientists, educators, entertainers, and sometimes even religious leaders. But who is reliable, who can we trust? Shortly before he died, Einstein wrote a letter to a friend in which he said, 'The need of the world is to listen to God.' But the question is, does God have anything to say, and if he does, how can we find out what it is. We might also add another question, 'Does God care?'

One of the major expressions of care is communication and the Bible makes it quite clear that because God cares he has communicated with us. In the New Testament we read that, *'In the past God spoke to our forefathers through the prophets at many times and in various ways, but in these last days he has spoken to us by His Son.' (Heb. 1:1,2.)*

Genesis is the first book in the Bible, and in the first chapter we have a record of the various stages of creation. One very interesting phrase comes before every stage of creation and it is, *'And God said.'* It is the first revelation given to us of the character of God in the Bible, and it tells us that He is a God who speaks, and his voice is a voice of power and creation. Something always happens when God speaks.

In the second book of the Bible *(Exodus)* we have the record of the Ten Commandments as given by God to Moses on Mount Sinai. As we saw in a previous chapter, these Commandments were not the result of a committee discussion and then a majority vote. Nor were they man's considered opinion as to what might be a good standard of moral behaviour for the human race, they were given by God's spoken word.

God also spoke through what the Bible describes as prophets, and they lived through many centuries in the past. Whether they stood before Kings or the nation of Israel there was one phrase that was always upon their lips and it was, *'This is what the Lord says.'*

But the verse in Hebrews 1 tells us that the God who had not been silent in times past, has in these last days spoken unto us by His Son. God's last word to our world is in Jesus. God spoke to the world through the birth of Jesus, because it divides human history in half. There is also no question but that the life of Jesus was unique in every way, and even his enemies in the end had to hire false witnesses to testify against him at his trial. On the mount of transfiguration, God spoke with a voice from heaven and said, *'This is my Son, whom I love; with him I am well pleased. Listen to him.' (Matt. 17:5.)*

For when Jesus speaks, God is speaking. So if you want to hear what God has to say, then listen to the voice of Jesus.

Amongst many things that Jesus had to say to us was a very straight statement, *'Except you repent, you will perish.' (Luke 13:3.)* and of course the opposite is true, if you do repent, you will be saved. So over the next few pages I want you to see how important it is to repent of your sin, because unless you do, you will meet God as your Judge and you will perish.

If you could speak with my wife she would confirm that I don't like gardening. But I have discovered one very basic law of the garden, and it is that what you sow you reap. If you sow carrot seeds you will grow carrots. If you plant tomato plants you look eventually for a crop of tomatoes. Equally if you neglect your garden, you will speedily find it overgrown with weeds, thorns and thistles. This is not only a natural law of nature that we can observe nearly every day, but it is also a spiritual law as well. The Bible says, *'Do not be deceived: God cannot be mocked A man reaps what he sows. The one who sows to please his sinful nature, from that nature will reap destruction; the one who sows to please the Spirit, from the Spirit will reap eternal life.' (Gal 6:7,8.)* The words of Jesus about the necessity to repent is one application of this moral and spiritual law.

So what is repentance?

It might first of all be sensible to spell out what it isn't. I remember hearing the story of the man who cheated on his income tax return and found that he could not sleep at night because of a guilty conscience. In desperation he sat down and wrote to the Inland Revenue enclosing a cheque for £150 and adding. 'If I still can't sleep, I'll send you the rest!' That is obviously not what the Bible means by repentance. Mere sorrow which even weeps and sobs is still not repentance, for repentance is sorrow that leads to action. It certainly is not reformation, penitence or just feeling sorry. It is not joining the church, reading the Bible, praying, or even believing certain facts about Christ, as important as some of these things are in the right place.

So what is it? Repentance is not a meritorious act or a wrought up temperamental or emotional experience. It is a new attitude taken towards sin and God, which results in a willingness to turn from your sin to God. Or to put it in the words of the schoolboy who was asked to define repentance, 'It's being sorry enough about my sin to quit it.' The Kekchi Indians of Guatemala describe it as 'it pains my heart.' Baouli people in West Africa are more precise. They describe repentance as 'it hurts so much I want to die.' William Gurnall says of repentance that it is ' to forsake and leave your sin without any thought of returning to it again,' for repentance is an attitude that leads to action.

In the Old Testament it says, *'Seek the Lord while he may be found, call on him while he is near. Let the wicked forsake his way and the evil man his thoughts and let him return unto the Lord and he will have mercy on him, and to our God for he will freely pardon.' (Isaiah 55:6, 7.)*

Matthew in his gospel says that *'from that time (after his baptism) Jesus began to preach, 'Repent for the Kingdom of Heaven is near.' (Matt 4:17)* The commission Jesus gave to his disciples was to go and preach that men should repent. Peter's message on the Day of Pentecost was *'Repent and be baptised every one of you, in the name of Jesus Christ so that your sins may be forgiven.' (Acts 2:8)* The whole New Testament echoes with the call for men and women to repent and to trust Christ as their Saviour, for *'Except you repent, you will perish.'* Repentance is the only gate through which the gospel of forgiveness is received. But it is also the golden key that opens the palace of eternity. It was A.W.Tozer who said that 'God will take nine steps towards us, but he will not take the tenth. He will incline us to repent, but he cannot do our repenting for us.'

So what happens when a person repents ?
Basically there are three elements in genuine repentance and it starts with a change of mind. Jesus told a story to illustrate this aspect of repentance and it is found in *Matt.21:28,29. "There was a certain man who had two sons. He*

went to the first and said "Son go and work today in the vineyard." 'I will not' he answered, 'but later changed his mind and went" and this is precisely what Peter called his Jewish hearers to do on the Day of Pentecost. They must change their minds and confess that Jesus was indeed the promised Messiah and the Saviour of the world. God also calls you to such a response if you would become a Christian - you need a change of mind. From a change of mind you also need a change of feeling. There must be a stirring of the emotions and feelings, so don't decry emotion. People get emotional reading a book or watching a film, and there is certainly plenty of emotion at sports events, so why not in the greatest upheaval in a man or woman's life. It is with the passions and emotions that men and women go into sin, so why should they not be involved in a person turning from sin to God. David the Psalmist says, *'I am about to fall, and my pain is ever with me. I confess my iniquity ; I am troubled by my sin.' (Psalm 38:18)*

So repentance is a change of mind, followed by a change of feeling, and then lastly there must be a change of action. There does have to be a strong desire to be different and to go God's way. There must be a willingness to surrender to the will of God. David in *Psalm 51:10 prayed, 'Create in me a pure heart, O God, and renew a right spirit within me.'*

Now all of these three aspects of repentance are vividly illustrated in the story of the Prodigal Son that Jesus told in the Gospel of Luke. *'There was a man who had two sons. The younger one said to his father. 'Father, give me my share of the estate'. So he divided the property between them. Not long after that, the younger son got together all that he had, set off for a distant country and there squandered his wealth in wild living. After he had spent everything, there was a severe famine in that country and he began to be in need. So he went and hired himself out to a citizen of that country, who sent him to his field to feed pigs. He longed to fill his stomach with the pods that the pigs were eating, but no one gave him anything. When he came to his senses he said, "How many of my Father's hired men have food to spare, and here I am starving to death ! I will set out and go back to my Father and say to him : Father, I have sinned against Heaven and against you. I am no longer worthy to be called your son; make me like one of your hired men'. So he got up and went back to his father.' (Luke 15:13-20.)* This young man had a change of mind that was accompanied by a change of feeling, and the both then led to a change of action, and this is precisely what God calls you to do. He calls you to confess and forsake your sin. You must stop going your own way and turn and go God's way, for *'except you repent you will perish.'*

The call to repent is urgent.

Before His ascension into heaven, Jesus appeared many times to his disciples, and on one occasion he told them *'This is what is written: the Christ will suffer and rise from the dead on the third day. And repentance and forgiveness of sins will be preached in his name to all nations.' (Luke 24:6, 47.)* The Bible makes it quite clear that repentance is not an optional extra or just a suggestion from God, but rather a divine command. Paul preaching in Athens on Mars Hill concluded his message by saying, *'In the past God overlooked such ignorance, but now commands all people everywhere to repent. For he has set a day when he will judge the world with justice by that man he has appointed.'(Acts 17:30.)* But this is no hard, unbending message. God is not trying to hit you with a big stick. Paul says, *'Do you show contempt for the riches of his kindness, tolerance and patience, not realising that God's kindness leads you to repentance.' (Rom. 2:4.)* And hasn't God been good to you in so many ways ? Peter reminds us that *'The Lord is not slow in keeping his promise as some understand slowness. He is patient with you, not wanting anyone to perish, but everyone to come to repentance'. (2 Peter 3:9)* Charles Colson of Watergate infamy said, 'When we comprehend our own nature, repentance is no dry doctrine. It is no frightening message, no morbid form of self flagellation. It is, as the early church fathers said, a gift that God grants which leads to life.'

Repentance is an initial element of saving faith, but it cannot be fully explained as simply another word for believing. As used in the New Testament it always speaks of a change of purpose and a turning from sin. More specifically, repentance calls for the repudiation of the old life and a turning to God for salvation. For repentance in saving faith involves three elements; a turning to God, a turning from sin, and an intent, a desire to please and serve God. No change of mind can be called repentance without all three. It is not merely being ashamed or sorry over sin, although genuine repentance always involves an element of remorse. It is a redirection of the human will, and a powerful decision to forsake all unrighteousness and to pursue righteousness instead. American author Philip Yancey tells the story of a group of Christian leaders who were invited to the Soviet Union in 1991. During the visit they unexpectedly met Nikolai Stalyarov the former vice-chairman of the K.G.B. During the time they spent with him he made a startling confession when he said, Political questions cannot be decided until there is a sincere repentance of our sins and a return to faith by our people. I have been a member of the party for 20 years, and in my studies of scientific atheism I was taught that Christianity divides people. Now I see the opposite-love for God only unites. The time has come for us to repent of the past.' (Praying with the K.G.B, Philip Yancey. Zondervan Press.)

But if you do repent the Bible says that *'there is joy in Heaven over one sinner who repents.'(Luke 15:7.)* Repentant sinners meet God without fear, because repentance is the entrance into the presence of God. However you do need to be aware of the danger of procrastination. If God's time (now) is too soon for your repentance, beware lest your time is too late for his acceptance. As Isaac Watts the hymn writer says, 'There is no repentance in the grave.' Those who wait to repent until the eleventh hour, often die at 10.59 ! You cannot repent too soon, because you do not know how soon it may be too late.

CHAPTER EIGHT

Meet God Through Faith and Find Freedom

For many people in the world today, God is an unfamiliar blur, they deny his relevance and in practice live as atheists.

A university student once asked the philosopher Hegel to explain a passage he had written in one of his books. Hegel read it and then said, 'When that was written, there were two of us who knew its meaning - God and me. Now alas, there is only one. That is God, and I don't know where he is.'

Then of course there is no question but that agnosticism and unbelief abound. Julian Huxley said with his usual anti-supernatural bias, 'I cannot see a shadow of evidence that there is a God.'

I remember a few years ago being involved with an evangelistic mission in a church that had several doctors in its membership. For five consecutive nights they invited 60 patients to come to the surgery as their guests. Coffee was served, then one member of the evangelistic team shared with them the relevance of the Christian faith for today. At the end of the week, the doctors gave us the background to these remarkable meetings, and without divulging any confidences said that the people they had invited were those that they felt had a spiritual problem in their lives rather than a medical one !

God shaped blank

Einstein was surely right when he said, 'The need of the world is to restore God to the centre of its thinking.' So could this be your greatest need ? You have a God shaped blank in your life and you are incomplete without Him - you need to meet God. Leighton Ford said that, 'Belief is not faith without evidence, but commitment without reservation. Saving faith is not creative, but receptive. It does not make salvation, but it does accept it gratefully. You can do a great deal without faith, but nothing that pleases God.' It was Arthur Constance who said, 'Saving faith is not the human contribution of a sinner seeking salvation, but the divine contribution of the gracious God seeking a sinner'.

But you say, 'What is God like, this God that so many Christians say they believe in and have a relationship with?' Man through the centuries has sought to conceive ideas about God. World religions give concrete examples of man's ideas about God and what he thinks is the way to find God and please Him. Some have tried to fashion God out of a tree trunk and others have sought to capture Him in marble or paint. For others in our Western culture, God is thought of as the man upstairs waiting to answer their every beck and call. But the God of the Bible is not an international slot machine into which we put our pitiful little offerings with the expectation of divine blessing. He is someone far greater and more wonderful than that caricature that so many people have in their minds.

So what is He like ? Where can we meet Him ? What does it mean to believe in him? I would suggest to you that the first place to look is in the Bible, the reason being that the Bible claims to be the revelation of God. If we are honest searchers for the truth and we want to discover the reality of faith for ourselves then we should be prepared to look at the source book of the Christian faith-the Bible

What Jesus claims.

One of the great accusations levelled against the Christian faith is that it is unrelated to life as it really is. Christianity, says the atheist, is all in the world of the unreal, fantasy and illusion. But nothing could be further from the truth. Real Biblical Christianity provides an answer to the deepest questions and needs of the human heart. Christian faith is experimental and proveable, and it can be shown to work in the 21st century, for at its centre stands a person -Jesus Christ. Jesus not only made claims concerning His own identity, but also claims about what He could do for people. For example Jesus said, *I am the way, the truth and the life, nobody comes to God except by me.' (John 14:6)* Thousands of people through the centuries have tested that claim; have come that way, and have found God. On another occasion Jesus said, *'I am the gate, by me if any man enters in he shall be saved'. (John 10:9.)* As with the first claim, many individuals have come through the gate of personal faith in Christ and have found salvation and forgiveness. Jesus said, *'Come unto me and I will give you rest.' (Matt. 11:29.)* Many weary, troubled and perplexed people have come to him and have found rest. Sir James Simpson the discoverer of chloroform for anaesthetics was once asked at a conference, 'What is your greatest discovery?' His reply startled his audience for he said, 'My greatest discovery was of Jesus Christ as the one who could meet all of my need and give me rest.'

The International thirst for freedom.

There is no question but that man around the world has an insatiable thirst for freedom. Politically and economically he wants to be free. Over the past few decades we have witnessed great upheavals in many of the world's great nations and their political systems. On the night when the slaves were set free in Jamaica in 1833, a large mahogany coffin was made and a grave was dug. Into that coffin the liberated slaves threw the reminders of their former life of slavery. There were whips, torture irons, branding irons, coarse frocks and shirts, large hats, fragments of a treadmill, and handcuffs.

Then the lid of the coffin was screwed down. At the stroke of midnight the coffin was lowered into the grave and buried. The liberated slaves sang the doxology, 'Praise God, from whom all blessings flow, Praise Him, all creatures here below, Praise Him above, ye heavenly host, Praise Father, Son and Holy Ghost.' But alas there are parts of our world where men and women are still not free.

In our day and generation in the Western World there is a great thirst for a 'permissive freedom' in terms of sexual morality. Absolutes are constantly being thrown overboard and situational ethics are substituted. If I want to do it then it must be right for me. Somehow or other within all of us is the urge to fling off restraint and to do our own thing. But of course this is nothing new. There has always been a seed in human nature that doesn't want to acknowledge God's authority. Adam and Eve started the ball rolling in the

Garden of Eden and the human race has gone that way ever since. But alas the end product is not freedom as we imagined it would be, but bondage. Albert Einstein said, 'The true problem lies in the hearts and thoughts of men. What terrifies us is not the explosive force of the atomic bomb, but the power of wickedness in the human heart.'

Because we were created in the image of God, we were designed to enjoy the company of our Maker. Our instincts will not easily allow us to forget our origin. However, our antagonism and state of enmity with God makes us a mass of contradictions. For humanity is not only at war with God. History all too frequently has shown us to be at war with our neighbour, with our environment, with our family and with ourselves. Our problems do not stem so much from our outward circumstances as from our inner state. True identity and significance continue to elude all those who do not know God, hence the symptoms of disorder. Humanity has great potential for creativity and technical advance, but when this is not controlled by a God centred view of the world then indiscipline and slavery are the result.

We do look for meaning and purpose, and freedom from fear and the sins that so often enslave us, but sad to say, what so often is on offer as the answer is totally unsatisfying. Richard Halverson said,' Man is a dust-bound god trapped by the instincts of his creaturehood. Man has power and he is mightier than Thor with his hammer. His rockets ride their shafts into the heavens and his atomic gadgets cause proud cities to tremble. But he is still man, able to take the town, but unable to contend and rule his own spirit, for man is free and yet not free.' Human nature is still the biggest problem in the world.

Immanuel Kant the German philosopher said that 'Freedom is the birthright of man. It belongs to him by right of his humanity.' But this is not true in experience. Man is a slave by nature because he serves his own lusts and desires. Seneca the Greek philosopher said, 'All of my life I have been trying to climb out of the pit of my besetting sins and I cannot do it' -and neither can you.

However, freedom as most people envisage it can be a most unsatisfactory experience as Solomon in the Bible discovered. He was King in Israel after David and he authored three books in the Bible. One of them was Ecclesiastes, and it is really a diary of his search for freedom in the various experiences of life. He travelled down many roads, but eventually he had to write *'Everything is meaningless.' (Eccl. 1:22.)*

He was probably the richest man in the world, and there is a lot that you can do with money. He built fleets and docks to service them in. Fortresses were erected all over the country and the Temple in Jerusalem named after him became one of the wonders of the ancient world. In his diary he wrote, *'I amassed silver and gold for myself and the treasures of kings and princes. But everything was meaningless, a chasing after the wind, nothing was gained under the sun'. (Ecc.2:8-ll.)* Our high standard of living today makes the luxuries of yesterday become the necessities of to-day. As one man said,' Let us be happy and live within our means, even if we have to borrow money to do it!'

Possessions cannot talk to you, love you, or guide you! Either their pleasing beauty wears off, or your eyes will grow dim to their lustre before you are eventually blinded by death. Those who live for money spend the first half of their lives getting all they can from everybody else, and the last half trying to keep everybody else from getting what they have away from them, and they find no pleasure in either half ! Former Beatle drummer Ringo Starr said on one occasion that he had almost everything that money could buy, and then he added, 'But when you can do that, the things that money can buy mean nothing after a while'.

However, there is a freedom that is an unqualified success. It is the freedom and release that can be discovered and enjoyed in Jesus Christ, for the Bible says, *'If the Son sets you free, then you are free indeed.' (John 8:36.)* Jesus alone is the answer to man's search for freedom. You see the reason why man is not free is because he has got a problem, and we have been talking about this problem in the previous chapters. It is not the problem of his circumstances, environment or even country of origin. Man has the problem within himself, and the Bible is the only book in the world that accurately describes the problem for what it is, plus giving the remedy that is totally successful. So let me turn you to a very important statement in the Bible. *'Everyone who sins breaks the law, in fact sin is lawlessness.' (1 John3:4.)* Here is a definition of what sin is -it is transgression of God's law. It also tells me that acts of sin bring me into bondage. *'He who does what is sinful is of the devil.'* But John goes on to tell us that *'The reason the Son of God appeared was to destroy the devil 's work.' (I John 3:8).*

Deliverance from sin comes only in Christ. It comes not because of the life of Christ, the teachings of Christ, nor even the example of Christ, but because of the death and resurrection of Christ. When the angels spoke to the shepherds in the fields below Bethlehem, the message was *'Unto you is born this day in the city of David a Saviour, and he is Christ the Lord'. (Luke 2 :11.)* Jesus when he began his ministry said, *'I am come to seek and to save that which was lost.' (Luke 19:10.)* Paul the great Christian preacher in the early days of the church said, *'Christ Jesus came into the world to save sinners.' (1 Tim 1:15.)* You are a sinner, so Christ came to save you . Jesus Christ is alive and he can come into your heart and life and set you free. Do you have this freedom? Has Jesus Christ set you free? *'If the Son sets you free, you will be free indeed'* - for in being set free you will meet God.

CHAPTER NINE

Meet God in Suffering

Suffering is sadly one of the facts of life that we wish was a fantasy, but usually seems to be part of our lives, and few of us escape it for very long. Reading the newspaper or watching the television news we are constantly bombarded with traumatic information about natural disasters, disease, famine, accidents, plus the sickness and pain that is the experience of the human race. Who of us can understand or handle the inhumanity of man to his fellow man? As human beings we cause pain when we are born. We then so often go on to inflict pain on others, and it is in pain that most of us die!

In the light of all of this heartache, it is no wonder that many people ask the question, 'Where is God in all of this suffering?' Is it really possible to believe in a God of love when there is so much misery in to-day's world? If God was good, would He not wish to make His creatures happy? If God was all powerful, surely He could change all of our bad experiences into good ones? But do the many good experiences of life when we are in health, strength and safety cause the majority to be thankful to God? No, most of us take it as some sort of right. C.S. Lewis in his inimitable way says that, 'The real problem is not why some pious believing people suffer, but why some do not.' If you are an atheist then you have no answer at all to the problem of suffering. You face all of the same questions and problems with me, but for you there are no possible answers. In fact you have no right to even ask the questions because there is no one there to answer them. The only answer that atheism can come up with in the face of suffering is 'hard luck, you drew the short straw.' As you read this chapter you may not find my explanation satisfactory, but at least with a belief in God, I do have an answer to give that countless thousands of believers in the world have found meaningful.

There is a suffering that can be explained.

According to C.S.Lewis, 'Four fifths of the suffering in the world is caused by man in a direct or indirect way.' It was men and not God who invented torture, the rack, prisons, concentration camps, slavery, guns, bayonets and bombs. It is men and women who exhibit avarice, greed, stupidity and exploitation. It is human beings who cheat, lie, murder and rape.

There is enough food on our planet to feed all of the world's population, but it is so often greed and man's exploitation of his fellow man that deprives so many of this God given provision. While some starve in the world, we in Great Britain spend millions of pounds on cat and dog food and the National Lottery. George Orwell said that 'most people get a fair amount of fun out of their lives, but on balance, life is full of suffering of one kind or another, and only the very young or the very foolish imagine otherwise.' Yes, many of the tragedies in life are man made in some way or other, but of course this would not be true of all of them. However the Christian faith does give us an explanation of how the universal tragedy of human pain and suffering had its beginning, and you can read about it in the first book of the Bible -Genesis. God created man in His own image. He then created woman from man and then gave them a beautiful world to live in and explore. God is a person, and human beings as the Bible says were created in God's image, and so had personality. God also gave to them a spiritual capacity to know Him and to enjoy a meaningful relationship with Him. But they decided that they would substitute self government for God's government, and what they thought was the pathway of freedom turned out to be the pathway of slavery, sin, pain and ultimate death. God put Adam and Eve in the Garden of Eden under moral constraint, but they decided deliberately to go against God's restraining hand. They substituted God's government by self government, and as a result, sin came into the world and the human race lost contact with God. The symptoms that followed that act of rebellion against God we are all familiar with, and they were blame shifting, self seeking, pride, rebellion, guilt, fear and lying. God created humanity in mint condition, but sin has vandalised us, for when humanity fell into sin, it lost itself. Any departure by man from what he knows he ought to do, however small his offence may be, slaps the very face of God.

Suffering in the world today in terms of man's inhumanity to man is the result of Adam's sin perpetrated by today's generation. You can blame Adam for starting the fire, but it is today's world that is piling on the fuel. So the origin of evil is a bigger problem for the atheist than the Christian. As a Christian I can account for evil and I do have an explanation for it that would seem to fit the facts of what is wrong with people and the world in which we live.

But suffering is not only physical.

There are of course different kinds of suffering and pain apart from the physical. I was reminded of this very vividly one night when sitting in a coffee bar and trying to be friendly with a teenager sitting rather quietly on his own. He said something to me that I will never forget. 'It will be lonely to be dead, but it could not be lonelier than being alive.' After I left him that evening I was reminded of a man in the Bible that Jesus met. He lived in Jerusalem and for 38 years had been a hopeless cripple. Most of his waking hours were spent by a pool named Bethesda.(You can read the story in John 5.) It was a pool that in Jewish tradition had healing powers when once in a while an angel troubled the waters. Whenever this happened, it was claimed that the first sick person to get into the water was healed. But as far as this man was concerned he had no one to help him into the pool and he was still in the same sorry condition.

One day, Jesus was in the city of Jerusalem, came past the pool, saw the man lying there, learnt that he had been in this condition for a long time and then asked him if he wanted to get well. But the only reply he got was, *'I have no one to help me into the pool.'* (John 5:7.) Or in other words he was saying, 'I'm on my own.' Here he was in the great city of Jerusalem with all of its teeming thousands of people, even very religious people, but he was alone.

I believe that the heart cry of this man, *'I have no one,'* is a cry that springs from the hearts of many people in our society today. Living in a crowd, surrounded by people and plenty of activity, but desperately lonely. For the strange paradox is that as our world grows even more crowded, we grow even more lonely. But loneliness does not always come from emptiness. Sometimes it is because we are too full - full of ourselves, full of distraction and activity. Paradoxically, I believe that if you want to heal the loneliness in your life, then you have to get to know God. We live in the day of the lonely crowd and there can sometimes be no greater suffering than loneliness. H.G.Wells on his 65th birthday said, 'I am lonely and have no peace,' Robert Perry said, 'There is a mystery in human hearts. Though we be encircled by a host of those who love us well, yet to every one of us from time to time there comes a sense of utter loneliness.' Smollett said,' I am sick of fame and lonely'. It is often the loneliness that some young people experience that makes them turn to the unreal escapism of drugs, alcohol, and sexual experimentation. Adam Faith, one time pop star turned actor and now a financial advisor said, 'When you are a teenager, you are not a kid and you are not an adult, you are an in between. You are confused and alone, and like a dying man, you are looking for an anchor'.

Sorrow, suffering and bereavement also bring their lonely experiences. 'I know how you feel,' says the friend-who calls to offer comfort when a loved one dies, but unless they have experienced what you are experiencing, they don't really understand. Who can comfort a mother whose baby has just died in her arms ? Then there are the long sleepless nights wracked with pain, and you begin to feel like that man by the pool of Bethesda in Jerusalem... *'I have no one.'*

Loneliness is one of those emotions that doesn't just exist by itself. It hitchhikes on guilt and depression. It is a parasite to lost emotions like fear and sadness. Unfortunately you can't buy anything over the counter at the chemist to cure it. You can't heal it by reading a book. You can't drive away from it in your car or hop on a plane and fly off to a new solution.

Wealth and fame can also bring their fair share of loneliness. It was the late Ernest Hemingway who said shortly before sadly taking his own life. 'I feel as if I am living in a vacuum that is as lonely as a radio tube when the batteries are dead and there is no current to plug into.' It was Carl Jung the psychologist who said, 'The pressures and problems of our complex society have produced a world of lonely people jammed together like sardines in a can we call earth'.

'Alone ! - that word, so idly spoken and so coldly heard
Yet, all that poets sing and grief hath known,
Of hopes laid waste, dwells in that word - alone.'

John Dominic Crossan shares his pessimistic view of the human condition in our post modern era when he says, 'There is no lighthouse or lighthouse keeper, in fact there is no dry land. There are only people living on rafts made from their own imagination -and there is sea...we are alone and lost.'

Then there are natural disasters.

Natural disasters as we often call them are of course a different story as they usually appear to be out of our control -although not always are we blameless. The Aberfan disaster in South Wales will still be vividly remembered by the older generation. A Coal Board tip slid away without warning, engulfed a school and smothered over 100 children. Sadly, the subsequent report into the disaster said that it could have been prevented. Man is often careless and certainly fallible. The terrible floods in Bangledesh that occur so often could be averted in some measure if the government and people would take the necessary measures suggested by the experts. The law of gravity that stops me soaring up into space is consistent when it also operates if I am foolish enough to step out of a tenth floor window. I cannot expect God to suddenly reverse His law for my personal benefit.

Earthquakes cause terrible destruction in some parts of the world, and sometimes bad building techniques and taking short cuts with sub-standard materials lead to an even larger loss of life than would have been the case. Science can tell us about the various plates' under the earth's surface that sometimes grind together and produce earthquakes, but science cannot tell me how they came to be as they are. But the Bible does give us a clue, because God's world created perfect in every way was violently turned inside out and upside down when the judgement of God was poured out on the world during the time of Noah and the worldwide flood. *Genesis 6:5* tells us that all of this came about because, *'The Lord saw how great man's wickedness on the earth had become, and that every inclination of the thoughts of his heart was only evil all the time. The Lord was grieved that He had made man on the earth, and his heart was filled with pain. So the Lord said, I will wipe mankind whom I have created from the face of the earth.'* Man's sin affected nature and the material world and we are from time to time reminded of this fact when natural disasters occur. It is God reminding us that we live in a fallen world.

But Christians also suffer.

Christians are also not immune from suffering, and sometimes they suffer more than non-Christians. The fact that there are Christians in to-day's world is proof that experiencing suffering and believing in a God of love are not mutually exclusive. Christians are also involved in war, pain, injustice, earthquakes and famine like any one else and yet they still believe that God is love. C.S.Lewis said that 'God whispers to us in our joys, speaks to us in our conscience, and shouts to us in our pain..' In our joy it is as though He is whispering in a crowded auditorium of His immense and outrageous love for us-but we can't hear. We are too busy and enmeshed with our friends, our joys and our lives. He sometimes speaks to us through our conscience, but we don't slow down enough to listen because our conscience's hearing aid is on low ! Without powerful listening, the communication process is not complete. But the 'Hound of Heaven' is persistent in his love and concern, so he shouts, and then sometimes through pain and suffering he has our attention.

Frank Retief said, 'Our sufferings are not always reasonable; probably one of the hardest aspects of suffering to endure is that it is not explained. It might be easier to bear if we knew why'.

Helen Keller lost both sight and hearing at 19 months old and was subsequently dumb as well as blind. But she learnt to read and lip feel and eventually graduated from Radcliffe College, Boston. Back in 1903 she wrote,' The world is full of suffering, but it is also full of the overcoming of it.' Leith Anderson said that, 'Adversity is often the window of opportunity for change. Few people or organisations want to change when there is prosperity and peace. Major changes are often only precipitated by necessity.

Joni Eareckson Tada at 17 years of age broke her neck in a diving accident. She has lived her life ever since in a wheelchair. But she has written a number of books, travelled the world, spoken to millions and touched more lives for good than ever she would have done if she had been able bodied. In her book 'Blessing,' Marty Craig describes how two of her four sons were born with severe abnormalities. She writes, 'In the teeth of the evidence I do not believe that any suffering is ultimately pointless or absurd, although it is often difficult to go on convincing oneself of this. At first we react with incredulity, anger and despair. Yet the value of suffering does not lie in the pain of it, but in what the sufferer makes of it. It is often in sorrow that we discover ourselves.' (Mary Craig. Blessings. Hodder and Stoughton.)

Reading the 28 chapters of the Acts of the Apostles in the Bible, you will find 56 references to Christians suffering. In the book of Hebrews in the New Testament and chapter eleven we read that some Christians were, *'tortured and refused to be released, so that they might gain a better resurrection. Others faced jeers and flogging, while still others were chained and put in prison. They were stoned; they were sawed in two: they were put to death by the sword they went about in sheepskins and goat skins, destitute, persecuted and mistreated.' (Hebrews 11:35-37)* During the reign of terror in Uganda under Idi Amin, over 500,000 Christians died. The World Christian Encyclopedia says that each year more than 30,000 Christians are killed for their faith somewhere in the world. Over the past 75 years there have been more Christian martyrs than in all of the previous centuries.

During the Simba rebellion in the Congo, thirty missionaries and their children were brutally murdered and thousands of national Christians suffered excruciating torture and death. In Sierra Leone there have over the past few years been hundreds of believers who have had hands amputated by the rebels - in one church over 50 men. Yes, Christians have known plenty about suffering but they are still Christians. But why is this so. Is there any explanation ? Yes, there is a reason.

God has suffered.

God in Christ experienced suffering, pain and loneliness of every conceivable kind. He knew the loneliness of leaving heaven's glory and coming into our world with all of its agony. Coming from heaven above to a manger in Bethlehem was a traumatic experience. His family situation was poor and on one occasion he said that *'Birds of the air had nests and the foxes had holes to go into, but he had nowhere to rest his head'. (Matt.8;20.)* His own people thought him strange and organised religion ostracised him. God in His mercy keeps us from knowing both the timing and the manner of our death, but Jesus knew both, and that must have produced tremendous emotional and mental suffering. In the Garden of Gethsamene his nearest disciples fell asleep and left him to agonise alone as he sweat as it were *'great drops of blood.'* Alone he stood as Judas betrayed him and all of his disciples forsook him and fled. In the Palace of the High Priest all condemned him. Pilate's Judgement Hall was no different, even though Pilate said that he found no fault in Jesus.

It was a lonely figure that walked, or rather stumbled those last painful steps up the hill outside the city wall. It was alone that He endured the beating, the scoffing, the nails in His hands and feet and the anguish of a Roman crucifixion. At the cross God is saying that He does care. He has experienced the loneliness and anguish of suffering, and He suffered all of this degradation and pain for you and me.

Eternity is the answer

A large part of the answer to the problem of suffering for the Christian lies in the sure knowledge that this life is not all. I am not just a pile of dirt swept under the carpet at the end of the journey of life. If that was the end of the road then there are far too many unanswered questions. But if there is life beyond the grave and that is certainly the teaching of the Bible and the Christian faith, then one day we shall have an answer to the questions about suffering.

If you try to find a watertight answer to all of the problems of suffering and pain you will search maybe for the rest of your life. But if you put your faith and trust in the living Lord Jesus Christ, then you will discover as have countless thousands around the world, an amazing experience of God's love and care for you. It may not necessarily rescue you from the pain and suffering, but it will certainly sustain you in the midst of it. You can meet God even in suffering. The poet R.S. Thomas said in a BBC interview, 'I am a Christian because I think Christianity gives to me the most profound and satisfying answer to the great problem of suffering. I don't think that even at this stage in our history that there is anything more contemporary than the cross. I would not be content to find an answer to the problem of suffering which did not involve God'.

CHAPTER TEN

Meet God and Find Peace

Joseph Conrad said that, 'What all men are after is peace,' and how right he was, for since the beginning of time man has been seeking for peace. Over the last 3000 years there have been over 5000 peace treaties, but most of them have been broken. During the past 150 years there have been 12 major wars, and since 1945 and the conclusion of the so called war to end wars, there have been local wars on nearly every continent of the world. We always seem to be on the precipice of yet another catastrophic war. A boy at school was asked by his teacher to define peace and his reply showed a maturity beyond his 12 years. 'Please sir,' he said, 'It's only a word in the dictionary!' - and he was not far out. Abraham Lincoln said, 'We must do all within our powers to achieve a just and lasting peace amongst ourselves and with all nations.' Presidents and Prime Ministers are still echoing his words but with little success. General George Marshall the instigator of the Marshall plan after World War Two said as far back as 1945, 'If man does find the solution for world peace, it will be the most revolutionary reversal of his record to date.' The world to-day is uncomfortably full of questions to which no man at present can return a sure answer, and of problems for which there is no quick and easy answer, and we long for peace.'

The human heart craves for peace.

There is not only a longing for peace internationally but also on the personal level. People need peace from a troubled conscience. I believe that all of us whether trained in moral and religious values or not, have God's moral code written within, and no technique on earth can totally delete or change it. When a man says that he has a clear conscience it often means that he has a bad memory. People want peace instead of worry, tension and fear, and nothing causes so much misery as uncertainty, and this is a very uncertain world in which to live.

So are you looking for peace? Maybe you have most things that our materialistic world can offer and yet you have no real peace of heart and mind, and you long for it.

You may even have sought to find peace in the church and religion, but so far they have eluded you.

But listen to what the Bible says in *Isaiah 26:3*. *'You will keep in perfect peace him whose mind is steadfast because he trusts in you.'* Here the Bible tells us that we can find peace as we meet God and make our peace with Him. So notice how this verse in the Bible starts. *'You will keep in perfect peace...'* The Old Testament was written in Hebrew, and the word *'Shalom'* is used for peace...and here in *Isaiah 26* it is used in a double way. In fact it could be translated peace, peace, instead of perfect peace. For God's peace once experienced can calm your heart and garrison your mind. The word *'shalom'* also has the meaning of health of spirit. Perfect peace then has spiritual health as its foundation. It is also the word used for peace in *Isaiah 48:18* where God says *'If only you had paid attention to my commands, your peace would have been like a river, your righteousness like the waves of the sea.'*

So here is the reason why so many are lacking peace, it is because they are spiritually unhealthy. We have a moral and spiritual disease that the Bible calls sin. Isaiah who spells out this message of peace says in the first chapter of his book, *'Why do you persist in rebellion ? Your whole head is injured, your whole heart afflicted from the sole of your foot to the top of your head there is no soundness - only wounds and welts and open sores, not cleansed or bandaged or soothed with oil.' (Isaiah 1:5, 6.)* .. and the divine commentary on the results of our condition is, *'Your iniquities have separated you from your God. Your sins have hidden his face from you.'* Sin is not only an offence which needs forgiving, it is a pollution which needs cleansing, for sin is man's declaration of independence of God. There is actually no such thing as a little sin, because there is no such person as a little God to sin against. It was Daniel Cawdray who said, 'A man may die as well by a fly choking him as by a lion devouring him'.. so likewise, little sins will sink a man to hell as soon as great sins. Sin does more than frustrate; it makes us fugitives from our destiny. Yet in our sinfulness, we remain plagued by a sense of homesickness. Nothing can ever relieve us of that pain, for where there is discord between God and man there can never be peace. Before you can know peace you must get right with God. You must get the sin question settled. But you can do nothing yourself about removing it.

But God has stepped in.

God has done something about our sin problem, and that is why Jesus Christ came just over 2000 years ago. He came on a rescue mission to remove the sin that separated us from God and kept us from peace. Jesus lived a life in obedience to God's law that we had broken. He said:, *'Do not think that I have come to abolish the law or the prophets; I have not come to abolish them but to fulfil them.' (Matt.5:17.)* But this alone could not bring us back to God, for God is righteous and sin must be punished. God does not let us off the hook, Paul writing to the Romans in Romans 5:8 says, *'But God demonstrates his own love for us in this, while we were still sinners, Christ died for us.'* It is only in the light of God's hatred of sin that we can really see God's love and appreciate the wonder of the gospel. The death of Christ was not the death of a martyr who was powerless to avert the fury of malicious man, nor was it the death of a tragic hero overtaken by an inescapable fate. It was the death of God incarnate.

Just as surely as there was an actual cross, body, blood, death and resurrection, so there was an actual atonement for sin and not merely the possibility of one. The death of Jesus Christ was an atonement which totally succeeded, and not an attempt which partially failed. It was Donald Grey Barnhouse who said, 'The cross of Jesus Christ is a two way street; we have been brought to God, and God has been brought to us.' The cross is the great dividing place for mankind, for at the cross God dealt with our sin. He made a way of forgiveness that we might meet Him without fear. If you will repent of your sin and surrender your life to Jesus Christ, you can have peace with God and then experience the peace of God flooding your heart and soul.

Listen to what the apostle Paul says in *Ephesians 2:13-17.'But now in Christ Jesus, you who once were far away, have been brought near through the blood of Christ. For he himself is our peace, who has made the two one and has destroyed the barrier, the dividing wall of hostility, by abolishing in his flesh the law with its commandments and regulations. His purpose was to create in himself one new man out of the two thus making peace. He came and preached peace to you who were far away and peace to those who were near. In Romans 14:17 Paul says, 'For the kingdom of God is not a matter of eating and drinking, but of righteousness, peace and joy in the Holy Spirit.*

It is perfect peace.

God's peace is first of all perfect in **'quality,'** for everything that God does and gives is perfect and not dependent upon our circumstances. It is then perfect in its **'quantity,'** because it can meet your every need. Paul in *Philippians 4:7* says. *'And the peace of God which transcends all understanding will guard your hearts and your minds in Christ Jesus.'* God's peace will protect your mind and calm your heart. But it is also perfect in its **'constancy.'** *Isaiah 26:3 says, 'You will keep in perfect peace.'* And this *'Peace of God that passes all understanding,'* can be your experience as well.

The gates of hell shall not prevail,
Or sputniks win the race
For God who made the heavens and earth
Is Lord of outer space.
No distance is too far for Him,
No man made bomb too great,
Yet pagan man with ruthless deeds
Connives to rule by hate.
The cross triumphant points the way,
.The crucified has won,
Not outer space, but inner peace
His gift when day is done.

Anon.

CHAPTER ELEVEN

Meet God at the Beginning of Life . . .

or a special word to teenagers

It was Solomon the ancient King of Israel who said in the Bible, *'Remember your Creator in the days of your youth,' (Ecc. 12, I.)* and possibly in a book that is full of good advice, this was the most important thing that he wrote, even though he waited until the last chapter to say it!

We live in a day when there is endless discussion about what makes a young person tick. Youth are constantly analysed, publicised, and without question endlessly criticised. Certainly the days of youth can be days of madness, when you 'tune in, turn on' then very sadly often 'drop out'. It is all too easy to go along with the crowd with a couldn't care less sort of attitude. They are also days when you begin to view the talent as far as the opposite sex is concerned, with all of its attendant problems. But for some there is the more serious side of life, when you are thinking and searching and asking questions about life and its meaning. 'Who am I? Where did I come from? Where am I going to?' We want to get involved in protest and social justice. The challenge of poverty in the Third Word challenges us to try and do something to help, even if only in a small way. But there is one important thing about you as a young person and that is - you are tomorrow. Teenagers today are to-morrows fathers and mothers, business men, teachers, community leaders, interplanetary travellers or tramps. You are potentially leaders of the future. In view of this, how important it is that now in the days of youth, you get to know God in a personal way in your life.

A Biblical example.

There was a young person in the Bible who lived in a complex, unhealthy society, facing many problems, yet he was someone who found God and found in Him the complete answer to all of his needs. His name was Josiah and his story is in 2 Chronicles chapter 34 in the Bible. At eight years of age he was crowned King in Jerusalem and after reigning for eight years, *'While he was still young, he began to seek after God.' (v.3;)* - and he went on to become one of the best Kings that the country ever had in its chequered history. All of this is rather staggering when you read the story and see what unhelpful influences surrounded him. His grandfather was a man named Manassah, and if ever there was a nasty piece of work it was this man. The Bible says of him that he reigned in Jerusalem for forty-five years and he followed detestable practices. He used sorcery, divination and witchcraft, and he even took a carved image that he had made and put it in God's Temple.

Amon was the father of Josiah and he was crowned King at twenty years of age, but he only lasted two years. His officials conspired against him and assassinated him in his palace, and then the people of the land killed the assassins and made Josiah king! Not the most helpful of backgrounds or start to life. But this teenager Josiah stood against the tide and came to a real personal relationship with God, and what a difference that made in his life and ultimately in the country that he was called to be King over.

You don't stand a chance.

Humanly speaking as a young person living in our pressure cooker society, you don't stand a chance of going the right way on your own and swimming against the tide. Within you is a heart and mind that so often thinks of all the wrong things. You have a will that directs you in the wrong direction and an imagination that sometimes frightens you. The explanation of the Bible about this problem is that, *'Within, out of the heart, come evil thoughts, sexual immorality, theft, murder, adultery and greed...all these evils come from inside and make a man unclean.' (Mark 7:21.)* Isaiah the prophet says, *'We all like sheep have gone astray, each of us has turned to his own way.' (Isaiah 53:6.)* You have a problem within, but there is also pressure from without. Friends are not always helpful and can pressure you to go the wrong way. There is the increasing propaganda of the media, literature, and the popular music world with its invitation to promiscuity. Artificial stimulants can easily get you hooked and lead to self destruction. You don't stand a chance with such a nature within and living in the world to-day.

But back to the Bible teenager Josiah

Notice what he did those many centuries ago and see how he coped with the situation that he found himself in. He did the **right thing,** for *'In the eighth year of his reign, while he was still young, he began to seek after God.'(2 Chron.34:3.)* Then he did the right thing at the **right time.** *'while he was still young.'* Life was in front of him. His character was pliable and still being fashioned. He was not yet set in his ways as an adult can be. Solomon was absolutely right when he said, *'Remember your Creator in the days of your youth.'(Eccl. 12:1.)* Lastly, he did the right thing, at the right time, but also in the *right way.* He repaired the house of God, the Temple. He instituted public worship again, and he gave God His rightful place. In effect what he was doing was renouncing the old way of life and embarking on a new way, and he was doing it publicly. Josiah was doing what the New Testament tells us that we all need to do if we would find God, and that is to repent of our sins. True repentance involves seeing sin for what it really is; not just a character defect, but a permanent posture of rebellion against the love and care and righteous authority of a holy God. It is a new understanding of God and of your own sin, and it will create in you a great desire to break with the past and to live in future only to please God and for His glory - (this is true repentance.)

There is also no question but that the days of youth are days of decision and commitment. If you are a teenager and coming near the end of school days you make a decision about university or a career. You may then fall in love and start a relationship that you hope might lead to marriage and eventually a family. But most of all you make the greatest commitment of your life as you face the challenge of Jesus Christ upon your life. In the days of youth you come to certain conclusions about God, the Bible, and the Christian faith. God speaks to you, convicts you, and calls you to come to Christ. But you do need to remember that Jesus said, *'No one can come to me unless the Father who sent me draws him.' (John 6:43.)* (If you do come to Christ, it is God who has drawn you.)

It was the choice that confronted Adam and Eve in the Garden of Eden. God's way was not to eat of the forbidden fruit. Their decision was to ignore

God's Word and authority and to substitute their own authority, and this attitude has been deep in the heart of human nature ever since. We substitute self-government for God's government in so many areas of our lives.

Moses put the challenge of this choice to the nation of Israel when he brought them out of slavery in Egypt and said to them. *'This day I call heaven and earth as witnesses against you, that I have set before you life and death, blessing and cursing. So choose life.' (Deut.30:19.)* Joshua said something similar a little later on in the history of Israel when he challenged them, *'Fear the Lord and serve him with faithfulness. Choose for yourselves this day whom you will serve.' (Joshua 25:15.)* Elijah the Old Testament prophet of God brought the challenge yet again when he said, *'How long will you waver between two opinions ? If the Lord is God follow him.' (1 Kings 18:21.)* Jesus certainly spelt out the challenge very clearly when he said, *'Enter through the narrow gate. For wide is the gate and broad is the road that leads to destruction.' (1Matt. 7:13.)* Josiah the teenager who lived so many years ago, did the right thing at the right time and in the right way. so what about you?

But you do need to win the sex battle.

Modern hedonism says that erotic love brings unending happiness. Choosing a wife is mainly selecting a good sex partner. If sexual attraction fades, divorce or affairs are permissible. However, this attitude deifies sex, making it an end in itself, an idol to be worshipped, and sadly, multitudes bow down at the shrine of sex as portrayed in this way. But this playboy attitude perverts true love which is other person centred. It overrides such qualities as loyalty, responsibility and consideration. It treats people as mere objects to be used for self gratification. God thought of sex before man did, and when man leaves God out of his sexual thinking, he is in real trouble, for sex is God's creation and gift. God created men and women and made them different. It was God our Creator who implanted physical attraction between the sexes. Sex is not sinful, and it can be accepted as one of God's gifts. But it is not a free for all, grab what you can while it is around. For as one of God's gifts, it is to be expressed in accordance with His design for it. But we do have to follow the Makers instructions, and those instructions are found in the Bible.

The Makers instructions.

It is here where Christianity differs from the philosophy which regards sex as only a natural impulse related to nothing ultimately but pleasure and self-gratification. G.K. Chesterton said, 'All healthy men, ancient and modern know that there is a certain fury in sex that we cannot afford to inflame, and that a certain mystery and awe must ever surround it if we are to remain sane.' So let me share with you a number of things about sex that are spelt out in the Makers instructions in the Bible.

- Sex is ordained by God to occur within the context of marriage. Extra-marital sex is out as far as God is concerned. Al Martin said, 'God never intended that man could find the true meaning of his sexuality in any other relationship than that of the total self-giving in marriage.' Marriage in the Bible is described as husband and wife becoming 'one flesh' and this physical union is too precious, too personal, too private to be used other than in the context of complete fidelity and permanence.
- Sex gives to a man and a woman a privilege that is denied to even angels, that of sharing with God in the making of a new life. It leads to parenthood, which gives love a visible continuity. Sex involves the entire life and personality, and to misuse it is to abuse yourself as well as your partner.
- It also relates to companionship. Eve was not given by God to Adam in the first place just for the propagation of the human race, but for friendship. When God created Eve He said, *'It is not good for man to be alone, I will make a helper suitable for him.' (Gen.2:15.)*
- Sex is also a physical unity which signifies something far deeper, because the Bible speaks of the 'two becoming one flesh. ' The meeting of two bodies cannot of itself express love, for love must exist between two persons before sex can manifest its God designed purpose. Loveless sex regards a person as a sexual object. It debases and destroys respect for others. Josh Mc.Dowell said, 'Love can wait to give; it is lust that can't wait, for lust is appetite run wild, and the world is littered with the debris of what 'Eros' has promised, but has been unable to deliver.'
- But sex is also for enjoyment. Nowhere does the Bible restrict sex to the sole purpose of procreation, for it was Solomon who said in *Eccl.9:9. 'Enjoy life with your wife who you love'*.

But sex outside of marriage is a no go area.

There are two words that the Bible uses for sex outside of marriage and they are the words 'adultery' and 'fornication,' adultery being sexual intercourse with the wife or husband of another, and fornication being illicit sexual intercourse with an unmarried person. The eye catching sight of an attractive girl is not wrong. But if we discover the impulse to lust through looking and cherish a sinful desire, this is mental adultery and as such is sin. In fact it was

Jesus who took the Commandment, *'You shall not commit adultery,'(Exodus 20:14)* from the realm of the act to the thought of the heart when he said, *'He that looks on a woman to lust after her, has committed adultery already in his heart.'(Matt.5:28)*

Todays obsession with sex certainly does present a real problem for the person who wants to stay clean and pure. If lustful looks were condemned by Jesus in His day, what sort of judgement would he pronounce on our society with its sick obsession with sex ? We live in an age when dirty or suggestive jokes are the norm. Nudity, pornography, filthy literature and vile videos and films abound on every hand. The Bible is so accurate when it says of humanity as far back as *Genesis 6:5. 'Every inclination of the thoughts of mans heart is only evil all of the time.'* The deification of sex, making it an end in itself, perverts true love. But the temptation, the pressure is strong.. so what is the answer ?

How to deal with sexual temptation.

In trying to find an answer, I want us to look at a story in the Bible. If you want to look it up and read it for yourself, you will find it in Genesis 39 in the Old Testament and it is the story of Joseph. Sold by his own brothers into slavery, he was finally bought in an Egyptian slave market by a high official and put in charge of his household, and it was in this situation that his master's wife tried to seduce him.

He was in his early twenties, so it was a time in life when he would have been particularly vulnerable. As he was a long way from home, no one would know if he succumbed. Yet, he faced this strong sexual temptation, resisted it, and came through victorious at the end. It was also a totally unexpected situation in which to be sexually tempted. He was busy in the routine of his daily duties in the house. So here is a warning that sexual temptation does not always come to us in a predictable way. Certainly his temptation came from an unexpected source in the person of his master's wife. It also came at a very favourable time. He just happened to be alone with her in the house.

But Joseph knew what was right and he also knew that to have given way would not only be a sin against himself and her, but most of all against God. His reply to her invitation was, *'How can I do this great wickedness and sin against God.' (Gen. 39:9.)*

Jesus said something in the Gospels that might on the surface seem rather drastic. *'If your right eye causes you to sin, gouge it out and throw it away. It is better for you to lose one part of your body than for your whole body to be thrown into hell.'* *(Matt.5:29)* What Jesus was saying in this radical statement was not for us to physically do this, but rather to make sure that we get rid of anything in our lives that would cause us to sin sexually.

Deliberate exposure to filth in literature, film, television or pop music lyrics can so easily lead you to mental adultery and will create in you an unhealthy thought life. Don't intentionally place yourself in the way of temptation. There is an old Chinese proverb that says, 'He who would not enter the room of sin must not sit at the door of temptation.' But of course there is only one ultimate answer and that is to make sure that you not only follow the Makers instructions regarding sex, but that you also get to know the Maker Himself.

CHAPTER TWELVE

Meet God in the Family

In our twentieth century society the family seems to be constantly under attack and certainly devalued. One local vicar in my home city said that in a three year period he had only conducted six weddings. Many couples just live with each other, and 'all change' is a not too infrequent experience In addition single parent families are an ever increasing phenomenon. So what is the value of family life in our world of today ? There are politicians today who would do anything to stop the 'M' word from even being mentioned in policy documents, but the argument for marriage is based on solid evidence which won't go away. The escalating cost of family disintegration - in terms of housing, social security, healthcare and crime-cannot be ignored. Nor can the fact that only 36% of children born to cohabiting parents are still cared for by both parents by the time the children are 16, compared with 70% of children born to married couples. Of course some children manage fine without two married parents, but to suggest that other types of family are just as successful for children is simply not true. The Government has no qualms about lecturing us to stop smoking and take more exercise. So why is it so reticent about the benefit of marriage ? Popular journalists and television comedians make jokes about marriage and treat it with some disdain. As one cynical disc jockey put it, 'Marriage is the most expensive way in the world to discover your faults. It is a school of experience where husband and wife are classmates.' Someone else has commented, 'That couples in our generation are married for better or for worse, but sadly not for long.' Engel the philosopher said, 'Marriage is an easily dissolved tie based only on love, with freedom for any other association without penalty'. A little girl came home from school one day really excited because she had heard the story of 'Snow White and the Seven Dwarfs' for the first time in her life. 'Tell me the story,' said her mother, and her daughter rapidly recounted the story right up to the handsome Prince kissing the sleeping Snow White and awoke her from her deep sleep. That was wonderful.' Said her mother, 'So did they live happily every after ? 'Oh no, said the little girl, 'They got married!'

But despite the cynics and the jokes, God is the author of marriage. It is not the invention of man as a convenient arrangement. Nor is it the end product of an evolutionary process in human relationships. The Bible says that in the beginning God said, *'It is not good for man to be alone, I will make an help meet for him.'(Gen.2:18.)* God then created Eve from Adam and gave her to him and said, *'Therefore shall a man leave his father and mother and shall cleave to his wife.' (Gen.2:24.)* Matthew Henry said,' God did not take the bone from Adam's foot that the woman might be beneath him. Nor did he take it from his head that she might be above him. He took it from his side that she might be protected by him.' So I think that we can safely say that God is a romantic ! Adam was first given Eve, not just to fill a natural sexual need, although this was recognised, but rather to fulfil his need for a 'helper,' and this is how Eve was described.

But what makes a successful marriage?

A successful marriage always involves a triangle - a man, a woman - and God, and the Bible makes it quite clear that *'marriage is honourable in all.' (Heb.13:4.)* It also very clearly spells out the responsibilities of both husband and wife in marriage. One of the mistakes of the women's rights movement is that although there were serious wrongs to correct, it then added to the problem. Instead of restoring women to their rightful place of authority beside man, women's rights became 'feminist' and this put women into competition with men. It led to the masculinisation of women and the feminism of men and ultimately to the unhappiness of both. *Paul in Ephesians 5:22-25,* says to wives, *'Submit yourselves unto your own husbands as unto the Lord'.* And then to husbands he says, *'Love your wives, as Christ also loved the church and gave himself for it.'* It was the late George Duncan who said that, 'The woman that rules the roost is on the wrong perch.'

But what about children ?

One of the greatest blessings in any marriage is the gift of children, and the Bible says that *'Sons are a heritage from the Lord and children a reward from him.' (Psalm 127:3)* We often start by calling them little angels, but sometimes quickly change our terminology when they start to grow up and get into scrapes, and sometimes don't really appreciate all that we do for them. One little boy was one day speaking with his teacher and saying that he was very concerned about his mum and dad, and his teacher was obviously keen to listen to what he had to say. The boy told him that his dad worked hard to provide for all of his sons needs. His mother slaved around the house, fed him, washed his clothes and took care of him when he was sick in bed. 'So what are you worried about,' asked his teacher ? I'm afraid they might escape,' he replied! Yes, as parents we do sometimes find that our children can take us for granted.

I remember hearing the definition of a boy that went like this. 'A boy is nature's answer to the false belief that there is no such think as perpetual motion. A boy can swim like a fish, run like a deer, climb like a squirrel, bellow like a bull, eat like a pig, or act like a mule. A boy is a piece of string stretched over an appetite. He is a growing child to be fed, watered and kept warm. He is a joy, a periodic nuisance, the problem of our time, but he is God's gift to you.'

Looking after them.

Parenthood, of course, as we all know, brings great responsibilities. Parents are to provide for their children, love them and train them, and there is no doubt but that being a parent is very hard work. The Bible says, *'Train up a child in the way he should go, and when he is old he will not turn from if.'* *(Prov.22:6)* The Duke of Wellington once said that if you train children apart from religion, you will only make them clever devils.' But as well as loving, providing and training them we are also to correct them when necessary - and correction is not very popular in some sociological circles today. The family is not only the first environment for a child, it is also the first school where it receives basic education. The very first form of government with which a human being comes in contact with is the government of the home, so how important it is that it is good government. The essential world for a small child is in the family with its mother and father in their rightful place. The apostle Paul said, *'Fathers do nor exasperate your children, instead bring them up in the training and instruction of the Lord.' (Eph.6:4.)* It was Henri Amiel who said that 'the true religion of a child depends on what its father and mother are, and not on just what they say. 'Every word and deed of a parent is a fibre woven into the character of a child that ultimately determines how that child fits into the fabric of society. Whatever parent gives his children good instruction, and sets them at the same time a bad example, may be considered as bringing them food in one hand and poison in the other.

Solomon reminds us that such training and instruction also includes chastisement when required, *'He who spares the rod hates his son, but he who loves him is careful to discipline.'(Prov. 13:24,)* Later on he enlarges on this further when he says, *'Do not withhold discipline from a child, if you punish him with the rod, he will not die. Punish him with the rod and save his soul from death. '(Prov 23:13.)* When a child begins to sow 'wild oats,' it is time for the father to start the 'threshing machine.' Whether parents resort to giving a pat on the back, low enough and hard enough, and often enough, or use a non -physical approach, the Bible demands discipline. The surest way to make it hard for children is to make it soft for them. Psychologists tell us that a child, for proper emotional growth, needs a structure of discipline to balance permissiveness. Children like flowers should not be crushed by mistreatment, nor allowed to grow wild. But I want you to notice that the Bible puts the major responsibility for such training upon the father, even if usually in practice it is mother who takes the major share in such training. The influence of a godly mother is of tremendous value. It is still true that the hand that rocks the cradle rules the world. Dr. Jowett said, 'Where there is a really great man there was first a great mother.' 'I remember my mother's prayers,' said St. Augustine, 'and if I am your child O God, it is because you gave me such a mother.' George Herbert said, 'The influence of a good mother is worth more than a thousand school teachers.' D.L.Moody the great American evangelist of the last century stated that 'All I have ever accomplished in my life I owe to my mother'. Being a mother, staying at home and caring for the children is not being a second class woman. It is a major investment in the lives of tomorrows generation and of paramount importance. Someone has so rightly said that 'our children need our presence more than they need our presents!' But one of the most challenging aspects of parenthood is that of realising that we are stewards of our children. God has given them to us on trust and although at the end of the day they will be individually answerable to God, yet as parents we are charged by God with laying down good spiritual foundations in their lives. It is not just up to them what they believe. Paul Helm said, 'It is emphatically not a Christian duty to let a child make up its own mind without informing, guiding and encouraging him. Christian parents should not inflict upon their children the cruelty of telling them that they should just do as they please.' Vance Havner the American preacher said, 'No man or woman ever had a nobler challenge or a higher privilege than to bring up a child for God, and whenever we slight that privilege or neglect that ministry for anything else, we will live to mourn it in heartache and grief.' I remember hearing the story of a doctor and his family who had to move into a hotel while their new home was being completed. One day a friend called to see them and was talking with the youngest daughter and saying what a pity it was that you don't have a home of your own. But the little girl quickly butted in and said, 'But we do have a home of our own, we just don't have a house to put it into yet!' Children need a home more than they need a house. You see, love is the master key to a happy home. Money can buy a house but it takes love to make it into a home.

Children's responsibilities.

Children of course have responsibilities before God in the context of the family. Once again Solomon speaking says, *'My son listen to your father's instructions and do not forsake your mother's teachings.' (Prov. 1:8.9.)* Turning to the New Testament Paul says, *'Children obey your parents in the Lord for this is right.'(Eph.6:I.)* To despise your parents, or to hate them and dishonour them is to despise the immediate source of your life. It is a form of self-hate, and it is a wilful contempt of the basic inheritance of your life. A teacher once asked his class to write out the Fifth Commandment, and one lad wrote, 'Humour your parents,' while another wrote, 'Honour your pirates! ' But while parents are not pirates, nor usually need humouring, certain obligations are binding on both parents and children.

Do you fit the picture?

So here is God's picture and plan for a happy harmonious family life. This is the family where there is joy, peace and mutual love and affection. But it is quite obvious that in many families something has gone wrong. There is quarrelling and bickering, unfaithfulness and broken relationships. Parents are letting their children down and children are disobedient and disrespectful to their parents. If our families are going to get sorted out and peace and harmony prevail, then somewhere along the line we need to meet up with God. One of the greatest benefits conferred on human beings, that of fatherhood, motherhood, childhood and home can become the greatest curse if God is not in His rightful place in the lives of all members of the family.

God is the author of family life and he knows how best to direct and control and enable us to find fulfilment whatever our role in the family may be. If this is true and it is, then the sooner we meet Him and relate to Him, the better it will be for us and our families. We need to meet God if we want to succeed in the context of our family life.

CHAPTER THIRTEEN

Meet God in the Bible

A few years ago I remember seeing a very simple yet eye catching advertisement for a British national newspaper. It contained only three words under the name of the paper - Readable - Reliable - Realistic. I am, not sure how accurate that was of the paper in question, but I was immediately reminded of how true that three word description was of the Bible.

It is certainly **readable** because its contents cover every taste in reading. There is history, mystery, archaeology, poetry, adventure and wisdom literature.

There is no question also that as far as scientific fact is concerned as distinct from scientific theory the Bible is totally **reliable**. John Blanchard in his book! 'Does God Believe in Atheists' (Evangelical Press) says that, 'True science and true religion have always been in perfect harmony with each other, and the Biblical theist celebrates science as a method God has given us to investigate the built in patterns of physical phenomena.' Albert Einstein could hardly have put it better when he said, 'Science without religion is lame; religion without science is blind'.

But maybe above all, the Bible is **realistic**. Through a unique collection of writings brought together over a period of about 1500 years, God has made plain his plan in this book for us citizens of planet earth, and he used men that he guided to convey his message. Some were chosen to write selected history and others to communicate wisdom and worship. Others unfolded the future, or gave instruction for belief and conduct. In fact every book in the Bible has its unique way of showing us God within the unity of the whole book. Brian Edwards says, 'God allowed these writers to use their own style, culture, gifts and character to write of their own experiences and to express what was in their mind, yet so overruled in the expression of thought and in the choice of words that they recorded accurately all that God wanted them to say, but in their own style and language.'(Nothing but the Truth'. Evangelical Press.)

The Bible reveals to us the way to God and the way of forgiveness and salvation It also reveals to us the way to find the will of God for our lives. But what is amazing is that although it has been attacked more than any other book, it is still according to the Daily Telegraph the world's best seller, selling over 20 million copies of the complete Bible each year and many more millions of parts of the Bible, such as the Gospels.

However more than its sale figures is the amazing way in which the Bible has had such a moral and spiritual influence on nations, communities and individual people all over the world. Even Immanuel Kant the philosopher had to say that 'the existence of the Bible is the greatest blessing which humanity has ever experienced.'

Most of the profound changes which took place in Great Britain in the 19th century were brought about by men and women who found their inspiration for social changes in the Bible. Amongst such people was William Wilberforce who campaigned against the slave trade, until eventually in 1807 it was abolished largely through his efforts. Elizabeth Fry was one of the first early pioneers of Prison Reform, and she was followed by Lord Shaftesbury in his tireless efforts to change the working conditions of people caught up in the Industrial Revolution. Thomas Barnardo was the initiator of homes for orphans and street children. During his lifetime, over 65,000 children had passed through his homes and many more thousands had been given material help. All of these remarkable people and many more acted as they did because of what the Bible meant to them.

Through the last few hundred years down to our day and generation, people's lives have also been transformed by the Bible. Emile Caillet the French philosopher who eventually settled in America received a secular education, but had always felt that something was missing in his life. He began to think that what he needed was a book that would understand him, but he knew of no such book, so he determined to write one for himself. As he came across moving passages in his studies he would copy them and then index his personal anthology so that when he felt despondent he could look up one of these choice passages.

The day came when Caillet finished his production and went out of the small town in which he and his wife lived, and sat down under a tree to read the book that would understand him. But as he read, a feeling of disappointment crept over him. The book did not work, because it carried no special strength of persuasion, and dejected he returned the book to his pocket.

At that moment his wife came up to him with a Bible. He had never read the Bible in his life, and his wife was almost afraid to give it to him, so insistent had he been about not having such a book in his house. But she had discovered a small Huguenot chapel earlier that morning and had asked for a Bible and been given one.

Caillet snatched up the book greedily and began to read it. Here is what happened as he wrote about it later. 'I read and read and read, now with an indescribable warmth surging up within. I could not find words to describe my awe and wonder, when suddenly the realisation dawned upon me: This was the book that could understand me ! I needed it so much, yet in my folly I had tried to write my own. I continued to read deeply into the night, mostly from the gospels, and lo and behold, as I looked through them, the One of whom they spoke, the one declared in them became alive to me. To this God I prayed that night, and the God who answered was the God of the Bible.' Emille Cailllet. Journey into Light. (Zondervan 1968)

But Caillet was not alone in discovering God through reading the Bible. A German missionary working in St. Petersburg in Russia employed two Mongol Tartars to assist him in preparing a translation of the four gospels into their language. They worked long hours over many months until at last the work was completed and the gospels were closed on the table in front of them. But still they sat, serious and silent. The missionary asked them the reason for their silence, and you can imagine his joy when they both confessed to having come to believe in the One who is at the centre of these gospels. One of them said, 'We have studied the sacred writings of the Chinese, and the more we read, the more obscure they seemed. The longer we have read and studied these gospels, the more simple and intelligible they have become, until at last it seemed as if Jesus Himself was talking to us.' It is interesting to notice that the Bible itself gives its own testimony to its effectiveness when read or heard, for it says, *'Faith comes from hearing the message, and the message is heard through the Word of God.' (Rom. 10: 1 7.)*

But does it work today?

A few years ago I was in Papua New Guinea with a camera crew and making a film to show the power of the Word of God coming to two groups of tribal people in this startlingly beautiful country. We reached the first group after a three and a half hours motor launch ride up two rivers. Missionaries had already reached them and shared with them the message of the Christian gospel. But now we had on board the first copies of the Gospel of Mark in their own language. It was fascinating and awesome to watch a group of men sitting on the river bank and holding in their hands for the first time a part of the Bible and beginning to read it out loud. One man with the gospel in his hand said to the missionary, 'Now we really do know that your message is true, because God speaks to us in this book.'

Down in the swampy lowlands in Western Papua we filmed another tribal group and spent some time talking with an old man who had been a tribal chief of what had been a cannibalistic tribe. This group had all originally lived in one long house for protection when other tribes attacked them. He said that there had been much fear and sadness and many fine young people had been killed. They had always lived also in fear of the spirits of the forest and the river. But it was obviously different now and I asked the old man what had happened, and his reply I will never forget, for he said, 'Then the Word of God came and our lives were changed on the inside.' Shakespeare or the writings of Karl Marx could never have done this -but the Bible could, because it is the Word of God.

It works for atheists.

For many years I have had the privilege of working with the church in some of the former East European communist countries. In one of them I had on many occasions preached with an excellent translator, a lady who taught English in an Institute of Higher Education. Talking with her on one occasion I asked her how she had become a Christian, and this is what she told me. ' It was in 1989 that a colleague of mine at the university told me something about the Bible for the first time in my life. Living and working in a tight communist State meant that I had very little contact with anything Christian. As my colleague had been in trouble many times for her faith, I was very careful how and when I spoke with her about God.

A few years earlier when working as an interpreter on a ship I had been given a small King James version of the Bible. So I went home, took the book from the shelf, and although the tiny letters were difficult to read, I started reading right from the beginning in the book of Genesis. I had of course heard about the story of Adam and Eve, but only thought of it as a religious myth. As for Jesus Christ, I had some vague ideas about him but not as a real historical figure.

But I started reading very carefully as if I was very thirsty. I never thought that it might not be true, I just swallowed the words and it was like finding another world. This Bible sounded like music to my ears and I understood almost everything that I read.

Winter and spring passed and I continued reading until I came to Solomon's building of the Temple in Jerusalem, but found this very difficult to understand, so decided to leave the Old Testament and start on the New. I had no difficulties whatsoever in understanding the Gospel of Matthew, and the Sermon on the Mount turned me upside down as I read these chapters over and over again until I could repeat them by heart. I was deeply moved and shaken in my inner self. All of my life I had lived in worry and fear, even though maybe I looked calm on the outside. The simple question of Jesus in Matt.6:27 asking if I could grow a bit taller by worrying about it made me realise the absurdity of my whole life.

Then I carried on and read Matthew's Gospel to the end. I was now not the same person and I knew it. My mind had been changed about God and Jesus Christ, but I was not impressed by the two gospels of Mark and Luke - they looked to me then as being basically the same as Matthew. So I started reading the Gospel of John, and as I read my heart was being changed and I was deeply affected. I remember sometimes nearly forgetting to breathe while I was reading. I continued reading what John had to say about Jesus and then by the last verse I realised that Jesus Christ was my Lord and my personal Saviour...and I began to jump for joy, for I had met God through His book, the Bible, and my life has been changed since that day'.

So it is still possible to meet God in the Bible as countless thousands of others have done through the centuries. It is not that the Bible as a revelation from God was designed to give us all the information that we might desire, nor to solve all of the questions that might perplex us, but rather to impart to us enough information to show us how we can meet God in Jesus Christ, and through Him to find forgiveness and salvation - so why not try it for yourself?

CHAPTER FOURTEEN

You Can Only Meet God on His Terms

In the book of Genesis, at the beginning of the Bible, is one of the saddest stories in the Bible. It is the story of Cain and Abel, the two sons of Adam and Eve. Both of them sought to meet God by bringing some offering to him, but one was rejected and the other accepted. The sad conclusion to the story as we shall see in a moment is that Cain (who brought the wrong offering) *'Went out from the presence of the Lord' (Gen.4:16)* He was a young man who had every spiritual opportunity and yet rejected them all. His is a story of disobedience, darkness, dishonesty, selfishness, unbelief and pride that ultimately led to his banishment from the presence of God. Yet what a privileged background Cain had along with his brother Abel, for they were the only children in the world whose parents had lived before sin arrived. Adam and Eve had lived in a world that was faultless and sinless, and a world where there was perfect harmony between them and their Creator. But as we know from these first few chapters of Genesis, they lost their unclouded relationship with God by an act of disobedience in taking of the forbidden fruit and so were cast out of the Garden of Eden. Paul in *Rom.5:12* reminds us that *'Therefore. just as sin entered the world through one man, and death through sin, and in this way death came to all men, because all have sinned'*.

The story of their act of disobedience in the Garden of Eden must have been recounted to these boys by their parents. They would also have been solemnly warned of the folly and terrible consequences of disobeying God. But they would also have been told that God had provided a way of reconciliation for them. It was the way of sacrifice. A lamb was taken and its blood (its life) shed as a substitute, an atonement for their sin. Maybe these boys had even seen their parents coming this way themselves, so they not only had the instructions by word of mouth, but also the visual aid as their parents came and met with God, and as a result were accepted by Him.

So it was that Cain and Abel grew up together with the same instruction and the same opportunity. But they made very different decisions, resulting in different destinies. *'Cain went out from the presence of the Lord into the land of wandering,' (Gen. 4:16.)* Maybe you have had the privilege of a Christian home. You were brought up in Sunday school, Bible class or the church. You have friends who are Christians, yet as far as you are concerned personally, up until this present moment of time, you have rejected God's salvation in Jesus Christ. Yours is still a story of disobedience, darkness, selfishness, pride, unbelief and unforgiven sin. You need to meet God in repentance, you need to come and trust Jesus Christ as your Saviour.

So let us look and see how this tragedy took place in Genesis 4. Abel was a shepherd, but Cain was what we might call to-day, a market gardener. The story tells us that *'In course of time Cain brought some of the fruits of the soil as an offering to the Lord. Abel also came with his offering, and it was a lamb from the flock' (Gen.4:3,4)* But then the Bible tells me that Abel's offering was accepted but the offering of Cain was rejected, and the question must be why ?

Why was Cain's offering rejected ?

Cain brought the fruit of the ground, and I am sure that it was first class produce, the best that he could produce as a skilled gardener. But God had cursed the ground after the fall and sin of Adam and Eve. God said to them, *'Cursed is the ground because of you; through painful toil you will eat of it all the days of your life. It will produce thorns and thistles for you, and you will eat the plants of the field. By the sweat of your brow you will eat your food until the day you return to the ground since from it you were taken.' (Gen.3:17-18.)* Cain brought the wrong offering. He brought that which God had cursed as far as a way of approach to him was concerned. God had made it quite clear that the right way was that of the lamb, the way of blood shed and life given as a substitute. But Cain thinks that he has a better way. He brought the wrong offering in the wrong way and certainly with the wrong attitude.

So it was that Cain turns from the revealed way to God to grope in the darkness of his own vain conceit. Cain was showing by his way of approach that he had no sense of sin, felt no need of forgiveness, and was certainly proud in his heart.

Could you possibly be making the same mistake as Cain. You are trying to come to God in your own way, the way of respectability, morality or even religion.. God has revealed the way through Jesus Christ, but you are still trying to come some other way. In the New Testament when Thomas came to Jesus with the all important question, *'How can we know the way'?* Jesus answered. *'I am the way and the truth and the life. No one comes to the Father except through me.' (John 14:5,6.)* Cain went out from the presence of the Lord, and so will you unless you meet up with God on His terms.

But God was gracious to Cain.

In spite of Cain's willful, proud and even disobedient approach, God gave Cain a second chance and said to him, *'Why is your face downcast ? If you do what is right, will you not be accepted ? But if you do not do what is right, sin is crouching at your door; it desires to have you, but you must master it.' (Gen.4:6.7.)* Is it not the same with you, for God has spoken to you on more than one occasion. In fact for you it might even be a second, third or fourth chance, and even as you are reading this, God is calling you to repent of your sins, to come to Christ and to seek salvation and forgiveness. If it is true, then I would urge you to take heed from this Old Testament story of Cain. Unbelief led to anger and then to murder, for Cain murdered his own brother. The tragedy of this story is that the first murder committed in human history was a man murdering his own brother!

Jesus would remind us that similar unbelief and rejection of God's only way of salvation will equally lead us to banishment from God's presence. *'If you don't believe that I am the one I claim to be, you will indeed die in your sins,' (John 8:21.)* said Jesus. It was A.W.Tozer who said, 'Every man will have to decide for himself whether or not he can afford the terrible luxury of unbelief. For unbelief is not failure in intellectual apprehension. It is disobedience in the presence of the clear commands of God.'

But what a tragedy.

For in the presence of the Lord was all that Cain needed, and of course all that you need as well. There was salvation and forgiveness found in the presence of the Lord. Salvation is found in no one else, *'For there is no other name under heaven given to men by which we must be saved' (Acts 4:12.)* Security is only found in the presence of the Lord, for God says *'I will let my people enjoy abundant peace and security. (Jer.33:6)*

There is also refreshment and joy in the presence of the Lord. Peter, preaching the first gospel message on the Day of Pentecost in Jerusalem said, *'Repent, then and turn to God, so that your sins may be wiped out, that times of refreshing may come from the Lord' (Acts 3:19.)* Are you looking for life, and for real joy! Then you will only find them in the Lord Jesus Christ. David the Psalmist said, *'You have made known to me the path of life; you will fill me with joy in your presence.' (Psalm 16;11.)* Dr. Norman Vincent Peale, a noted heretical famous American preacher recalls how when visiting a local hospital he met a girl badly crippled as a result of polio that had attacked her in her childhood. She always seemed to be cheerful and with a deep sense of joy that often radiated from her face. He asked her how on earth she could be like this when physically she was so weak. 'It is because I have God's telephone number', she replied. 'It is Jeremiah 33:3. and I found it in this directory,' pointing to a Bible beside her bed. Dr. Peale picked the Bible up and turned to the reference and read these words. 'Call to me and I will answer you and tell you great and unsearchable things you do not know'. And that Jeremiah number is available to you if you need it -24 hours a day - and it brings you directly into the presence of God.

Power is also discovered in the presence of the Lord. Isaiah the prophet says, *'Oh that you would rend the heavens and come down, that the mountains would tremble at your presence.' (Isaiah 64:1)* Do you need power in your life ? You only find it in the presence of the Lord. Cain went out from the presence of the Lord. But will you come into God's presence and meet Him on His terms ?

The New Testament tells us something very important about Abel. *'By faith Abel offered God a better sacrifice than Cain did. By faith he was commended as a righteous man, when God spoke well of his offering. And by faith he still speaks, even though he is dead.' (Heb. 11:4.)* His was an offering of faith and obedience, and God accepted him. God will also accept you if you come God's way - for this is the only way to meet him without fear.

Just as Abel brought a lamb as an atonement for his sin, so did Jesus the

Lamb of God make an atonement for your sins. In the Old Testament we are told that *'All we like sheep have gone astray, each of us has turned to his own way, and the Lord has laid on him the iniquity of us all.' (Isaiah 53:6)*

When we come to the New Testament we are told by way of explanation why Jesus died, and it was because *'He who knew nothing of sin was made sin for us.'(2 Cor.5:21.)* He came to bring the forgiveness and salvation that we all need, but it was exceedingly costly -not as far as we were concerned - but costly for God. It cost Him the death of His Son. But amazingly it is absolutely free to us if we will only receive it on God's terms and in His way, and in our last chapter we will see how we can make this true in our lives in a personal way.- so read on.

CHAPTER FIFTEEN

Meet God Now

Saved is a word that we are familiar with in every day language. It has the thought of rescue, help and deliverance. It speaks of a need that cannot be met by self- effort, and it conveys the idea of expertise that comes from an outside source. The hungry of the world cry out to be saved from starvation, and in some areas of the world there are still deadly diseases like malaria that kill thousands of people. Sadly there are also some countries of the world where people are slaves -and sold as such. But whenever there is a disaster in some part of the world, whether from earthquake, flood or famine, the more affluent nations of the world are usually urged to quickly respond to help those who have no possibility of helping themselves. So we understand what salvation means in these circumstances.

When you examine the Christian faith you will discover that it uses the word 'saved' or 'salvation' many times, but what does it mean in the Christian sense? In a letter in the New Testament written by Paul to Christians living in Rome he uses this word and says *'If you confess with your mouth Jesus is Lord, and believe in your heart that God raised him from the dead, you will be saved. For everyone who calls on the name of the Lord will be saved.'(Rom. 10:9-13)* But then having read these words you may be still no nearer knowing what the Bible means when it speaks of being saved.

Before Jesus was born an angel appeared to Joseph and gave him some very important pieces of information about the baby that Mary was carrying. He told him that the child was going to be a boy, and that He was to be called Jesus. Then he was given the reason why this baby was to be so named, *'For he will save his people from their sins.' (Matt. 1:21.)* For when the Bible uses the word salvation, it is talking about salvation from our sins, and in case we might think that is nothing to do with us, the Bible reminds us, *'All have sinned and come short of the glory of God.' (Rom 3:23.)* Sin is breaking God's law. ie. The Ten Commandments - and any one of them, for transgression of God's law is sin. In fact the Bible goes onto say *'For whoever keeps the whole law, and yet stumbles at just one point, is guilty of breaking all of it.' (James 2:10.)* Vague generalisations about sin are ineffective, we need specific admonitions and prohibitions and this is why God gave us His law. But sin is also omission, or failing to do the positive good, for the Bible says that *'to him who knows to do good and doesn't do it, to him it is sin.'* Jesus added one other condemnation when he said *'If you do not believe that I am the one I claim to be, you will indeed die in your sins.'(John 88:24.)*

Although we have been created by God and for Him, we have sadly left the path of obedience to God and stepped onto the path of personal independence from God. We have substituted God's government for self government, and that is sin. But without Him, life makes no sense at all. On our own we are unable to change our nature as the sin principle dominates us, and our actions and habits show that we are in slavery to sin. We live our lives under the shadow of death. As human beings we were made by God and for God and He gave to us a spiritual capacity. But we are far from God - yet we constantly search for our spiritual home and for an experience which materialism is unable to give us. What we need is the forgiveness of sins and an experience of God's salvation.

Because we have rejected God and followed our own way rather than God's we are guilty before him. Guilt is both a feeling and a fact. It is a feeling because our consciences tell us when we have done wrong. But it is also a fact, because God knows that we have rebelled against Him. We deserve God's judgement and we need to be saved, delivered and rescued from that judgement.

So who can be saved?

First of all we are told clearly in the Bible what the scope of God's salvation is, for it says very definitely that, *'Everyone who calls on the name of the Lord will be saved' (Rom.10:13.)* No matter what colour or race, good or bad, religious or pagan, young or old. It does not matter whether you have a little knowledge of the Bible or a lot, the invitation is *'Everyone who calls ... will be saved'*. The Bible says that *'God so loved the world that he gave his one and only Son, that whosoever believes in him shall nor perish but have eternal life.' (John 3:16.)* Paul in Romans 10: 12 says, *'The same Lord is rich unto all that call upon him.'* Peter writes in *2 Peter 3:9, 'God is not willing that any should perish, but that all should come to repentance.'* In *2 Cor.5:19* Paul says, *'God was reconciling the world to himself in Christ.'* God's salvation is for the world and therefore it is for you. No one can turn round and say, 'But it cannot possibly be for me.' To make such a statement is in effect to call God a liar, because he says that *'everyone who calls upon the name of the Lord will be saved'*.

Paul then underlines the source of this salvation and forgiveness. There is no salvation in politics, social reform or science, but only in Jesus Christ. It is not calling upon the name of the minister or priest. It is not calling upon the name of the church. It is calling upon the name of the Lord. Until the good news of salvation is received, a state of hostility exists between God and us. It is the death of Christ alone as we have already seen in previous chapters of this book that can change our situation. It is the cross alone that satisfies God's justice, for there God's anger against sin was fully poured out upon Jesus as our substitute. The way is now open for us as repentant sinners to 'call upon the name of the Lord' and so to receive the reconciliation and salvation made available for us in Jesus Christ. To save a single soul is beyond the combined resources of the world's banks or the skill of any top flight legal advocate. But call upon the name of the Lord and you will be saved. Some scientists believe that genetic manipulation holds promise for both the improvement and the destruction of human civilisation. By controlling genes which largely determine the physical and mental characteristics of a person, the scientists hope that one day they can create a perfect man. But to control or alter the physical and even mental characteristics of man is not enough to make a perfect man. For the Bible makes it quite clear that, 'Man's heart is deceitful and desperately wicked,' for at the heart of the human problem is the problem of the human heart, and only God can change us on the inside and give us a new heart.

Call upon the name of the Lord.

But why does it say 'call upon the name of the Lord'. In order to find an answer we must look at some other verses in the Bible that will help us in our understanding of why this phrase is used. In the Acts of the Apostles and right at the beginning of the Christian gospel, Peter and John heal a lame man at the beautiful gate of the temple. In healing him, Peter says, *'In the name of Jesus Christ of Nazareth rise up and walk.' (Acts 3:6.)* Later on when they are challenged by religious leaders as to how this miracle had happened they said, *'In the name of Jesus Christ does this man stand here whole.' (Acts 4:10.)* Peter then goes on to say, *'Neither is there salvation in any other, for there is none other name under heaven given among men whereby we must be saved.' (Acts 4:13.)* It was the late Lindsay Glegg who said that, 'There are many paths to Christ as there are feet to tread them. But there is only one way to God and that way is through Jesus Christ.' Now there are a number of reasons why the name of the Lord is so important. When you call upon the name of the Lord, you are calling upon God your Creator and lawgiver and the one that you have sinned against, for all sin is ultimately against God. But you are also calling upon the One whose name is Jesus. Do you remember what the angel said to Joseph about the baby that Mary was carrying. *'You will call his name Jesus, for he will save his people from their sins,'* for the Lord Jesus is the Saviour of sinners.

Then another title given to Jesus is -the Christ the Sent One - the Son of God, and the Bible often uses this title for Jesus. Paul in *Romans 5:8* says *'But God commendeth His love towards us in that while we were yet sinners, Christ died for us.' John in 1 John 4:14* echoes this truth when he writes, *'The Father sent the Son to be the Saviour of the world.'* So you can trust Him and his promises, for He is the Lord Jesus Christ.

But you do have to call.

It is very important to notice that this promise that emphasizes the importance of the *'the name of the Lord,'* also very clearly tells us that in order to enjoy this salvation we have to call for it. If you have an illness in the middle of the night you may need to call a doctor, for he certainly will not come if you don't telephone him and urge him to come and see you. If it is winter time and a frozen pipe bursts and water is spurting everywhere, you will need to call for the plumber. If your car breaks down on the motorway and you have renewed your AA Subscription, then you ring for help. There is no way that the AA will come to your rescue until you call. Now although God's salvation is universal in the sense that it is offered to the world, it is never bestowed automatically, there has to be a call to God for it, and such a call is only made when there is a sense of need. Jesus one day told a story about two men who prayed to God in the Jewish Temple because they wanted to be accepted by God. The first man was very religious and moral and as he prayed he told God how good he was compared to other men. The second man was just the opposite sort of character. He was at the bottom of the pile as far as religion and personal goodness was concerned. He came and prayed what I think is possibly the easiest and yet the hardest prayer to pray. He cried out to God and said,

'God be merciful to me a sinner.' He wasn't interested in comparing himself with any other human being, he just realised that as far as God was concerned he was a sinner. He also knew that if there was to be any mercy, forgiveness and salvation then only God could provide it, so he called. There was also a sense that he was coming in faith, believing that God could have mercy on him. Jesus added a wonderful encouraging postscript to the story when he said that this second man went down to his house right with God, forgiven and saved. *(See Luke 18:9-14.)* If at this moment you realise that you are a sinner and believe in your heart that Jesus Christ died for your sin on the cross, then call to Him to save you, and He will, for He promises, *'Everyone who calls on the name of the Lord will be saved.'* There are so many people who believe the great truths of the Christian faith. They realise that they are sinners and even believe that Christ died for their sins and that He is the only way of salvation, but the tragedy is that they have never called and so they are still unsaved because they have only believed in an intellectual way. Could that still be true of you?

Salvation is guaranteed.

This verse says very clearly that *'everyone who calls will be saved'.* It doesn't say, might be saved, or even stands a good chance of being saved. It states very clearly and dogmatically... *'will be saved.'* Jesus said *'Whoever hears my word and believes him who sent me has eternal life and will not be condemned; he has crossed over from death to life.' (John 5:24.)* God promises in the Bible that *'As far as the east is from the west, so far has he removed our transgressions from us.' (Psalm 103:12.)* If it had said as far as the north is from the south we would not be happy, because it is possible to measure the distance between the North and South Pole, but you cannot measure the distance between east and west.

Discovering and experiencing God's salvation in Jesus Christ brings salvation.

You are not saved because you attend church, are confirmed or baptized. You are not even saved if you live a respectable life or help your neighbour, but only if you have called upon the name of the Lord. Call to him now, *'God be merciful to me a sinner,'* and you will meet God, and then be assured as C.H. Spurgeon said, 'It is not your hold on Christ that saves you, but rather His hold on you.'

The Bible says, *'If you confess with your mouth, Jesus is Lord, and believe in your heart that God raised him from the dead, you will be saved. For it is with your heart that you believe and it is with your mouth that you confess and are saved.. for the Lord richly blesses all who call, for everyone who calls upon the name of the Lord will be saved' (Rom.10:9-13.) So MEET GOD.*

For more information, help or advice, you can contact the author, Peter Anderson

c/o
Ambassador Productions
Providence House
Ardenlee Street
Belfast
BT6 8QJ
Northern Ireland
U.K.